CAMMELL LAIRD

CAMMELL LAIRD

IAN COLLARD

Frontispiece: Mauretania *was one of the most famous ships built at Birkenhead.*

First published in 2004 by Tempus Publishing

Reprinted in 2012 by
The History Press
The Mill, Brimscombe Port,
Stroud, Gloucestershire, GL5 2QG
www.thehistorypress.co.uk

© Ian Collard, 2012

The right of Ian Collard to be identified as the Author
of this work has been asserted in accordance with the
Copyrights, Designs and Patents Act 1988.

British Library Cataloguing in Publication Data.
A catalogue record for this book is available from the British Library.

ISBN 978 0 7524 3267 0

Typesetting and origination by
Tempus Publishing Limited.
Printed in Great Britain.

Contents

Acknowledgements 6

Introduction 6

one History of the Yard 9

two The Ships 37

Acknowledgements

I wish to thank the staff at Wirral Archives – especially Colin Simpson and Emma Challinor – for their help and assistance and support. Without their help it would have not been possible to produce this work. Particular thanks must also go to Duncan Haws for the wealth of information gleaned from some of his major works on the history of the world's shipping companies.

Thanks also to *Marine News* which is the journal of the World Ship Society, and to Adrian Sweeney and the publication *Ships of Mann*. Gary Andrews, John Luxton and Trevor Kidd ensured that all the information in the work was completely up to date, accurate and correct. Stephen Card provided assistance, as well as his permission to include his painting of the Monarch of Bermuda and Queen of Bermuda.

A special thanks must go to the many people of Merseyside who worked at the yard over the years and were able to give me first-hand information and facts about the vessels that were built at Cammell Laird.

Introduction

Writing and compiling a book is like embarking on a voyage of discovery and this project has proved to be a positive learning exercise. I have lived on the Wirral all of my life and have always been aware of the tremendous benefit Cammell Laird's shipyard has brought to the social and economic fabric of the area.

It was one of those things that was always there and one that I assumed would survive the ravages of economic fortune and political change. The yard was the largest employer in the town and you always knew someone who worked there. It was so successful – even until recent times – that you assumed that it would adapt and change and survive.

However, when the orders ceased to come to the yard and overseas competition was so severe, even British ship-owners were forced to place contracts with European, Far Eastern and Japanese shipyards. Governments decided that it was more important to follow a strategy of 'high technology' employment and leave many of the traditional industries to other countries that were better prepared to succeed.

At the end of the twentieth century we also witnessed glasnost and the last period of the Cold War that brought about a rationalisation of the world's naval strength and commitments. Consequently, the yards like Cammell Laird that had moved to specialising in various naval vessels suffered when the size, type and numbers of naval ships were reduced, and only a few survived.

My first memory of Cammell Laird Shipyard was in 1959 when I went there to witness the launch of the Union Castle passenger liner, *Windsor Castle*, by Her Majesty Queen Elizabeth, the Queen Mother. I was at school and took an interest in the progress of the construction of the ship as she dominated the skyline of the town. I remember how we all took pride in the building of this massive and yet beautiful ocean liner and recall seeing her masts and funnel lifted into place while she lay in the wet basin.

Following her sea trials I discovered that she was open to inspection by the workers and their families prior to being handed over to her owners. I did not have a ticket but went along with some friends and told the man on the gate that I had mislaid mine. To my surprise he let me into the yard and onto the ship. I still recall wandering around that magnificent ship and standing high on the bridge wing, looking across the town and over the river.

I followed her down the river on the Wallasey ferry *Leasowe* when she moved to Gladstone Dock for her underwater inspection and painting, and waved to her from the beach at New Brighton when she sailed to Southampton to prepare for her maiden voyage to South Africa.

My interest in ships and shipping developed over the years and I was able to witness the naming and launching of many vessels that were built at the yard. In that period Cammell Laird were successful in gaining orders for a range of different types of ships, from ferries to tankers, cargo vessels, cable-ships, submarines and other naval vessels. The yard has been responsible for the construction of many famous, illustrious, legendary and well-known ships that have featured in the maritime and naval traditions of most of the major seagoing countries of the world.

In 1840 *Nemesis* was the first iron ship to round the Cape of Good Hope. Later that year it was involved in the Opium Wars off China. *Dover* was also built in 1840 and was the first iron ship to be owned by the British Government, and *Guadeloupe* was the largest iron ship to be built when she was completed at the yard in 1842.

HMS *Birkenhead* was credited with the term 'women and children first' when she collided with a rock off South Africa in 1852. The *Ma Robert* was a paddle steamer built for David Livingstone to sail up the Zambezi River. One of the most famous and notorious ships built at Birkenhead was the Confederate steamer, *Alabama*, which was completed in 1862 and sank twenty-seven ships in her first year in service.

In 1870 the yard delivered HMS *Captain*, a masted turret ship. She sank later that year with a loss of 480 lives when it was found that she was unstable. *Snowdrop* was built in 1910 for the Seacombe, Egremont and New Brighton ferry services and operated in Scotland

Keel of HMS Audacious.

until 1953, when she was broken up. HMS *Audacious* was the first major warship to be lost in the First World War when she struck a mine and sank off Malin Head in Northern Ireland. Her crew were transferred to the *Olympic* which was the sister ship of the *Titanic*.

Bergensfjord was built for the Norwegian America Line in 1913 and following service with various owners she was not withdrawn from service until 1959. Her near sister, *Stavangerfjord*, built in 1918, was not broken up until 1964. The passenger liner, *De Grasse*, was completed in 1924 and became the *Empress of Australia* when Canadian Pacific Steamships purchased her in 1953 as a replacement for the *Empress of Canada* which caught fire and capsized in Gladstone Dock, Liverpool.

HMS *Rodney*, completed in 1927, was in action with HMS *King George V* in May 1941 when they sank the *Bismarck*. HMS *Ark Royal* was launched at Birkenhead in 1937 and was the first British naval vessel to be designed and built as an aircraft carrier. She was involved in the pursuit of the German cruiser, *Graf Spee*, in 1939 and sank when a torpedo hit her in November 1941.

When her keel was laid at Birkenhead in 1937, *Mauretania* became the largest liner to be built in England and the first liner to be constructed for the Cunard–White Star Line. HMS *Thetis* sailed from Birkenhead on 1 June 1939 for sea trials and sank in Liverpool Bay with a loss of ninety-nine men.

The submarines HMS *Springer* and HMS *Sanguine* were 'S' Class vessels that became the largest group of submarines ever built for the Royal Navy and the yard completed thirty-five of these vessels. In 1958, *Springer* and *Sanguine* were sold to the Government of Israel and were given new Hebrew names by the first Prime Minister of Israel, Mr David Ben-Gurion.

The new aircraft carrier HMS *Ark Royal* was launched at the yard on 3 May 1950 and was handed over to the Royal Navy in 1955. She gave service to the country until she was broken up in 1980. *Manx Maid* was the first car ferry built for the Isle of Man Steam Packet Co. in 1962 and was followed by a sister ship, *Ben-My-Chree*, four years later.

Birkenhead Corporation ordered a new Mersey ferry which was named *Overchurch* in 1962 and is still maintaining the ferry service as *Royal Daffodil* in 2004. HMS *Devonshire* was a guided missile destroyer, built in 1962 to provide guided weapon anti-aircraft defence and anti-submarine duties.

The submarine HMS *Onyx* was completed in 1967 and was called into action in 1981 as part of the Falklands Task Force, where she was responsible for special operations roles and landed special forces to gather intelligence. Another Lairds-built submarine, HMS *Conqueror*, holds the distinction of being the only nuclear-powered submarine to have engaged the enemy with torpedoes in action when she hit the Argentine vessel *General Belgrano* on 30 April 1982. The Type 42 destroyer HMS *Coventry* was also a member of the Falklands Task Force when she was hit by Argentine Air Force A-4B Skyhawks and sank on 25 May 1982.

In September 1989 the submarine HMS *Unseen* was launched at Birkenhead. It was originally planned to construct twelve in this class; this was reduced to ten and following the 1990/91 Defence Review, it was cut to four vessels. The third vessel of this class, HMS *Unicorn*, became the last vessel to be built by Cammell Laird at Birkenhead.

Ian Collard,
October 2004

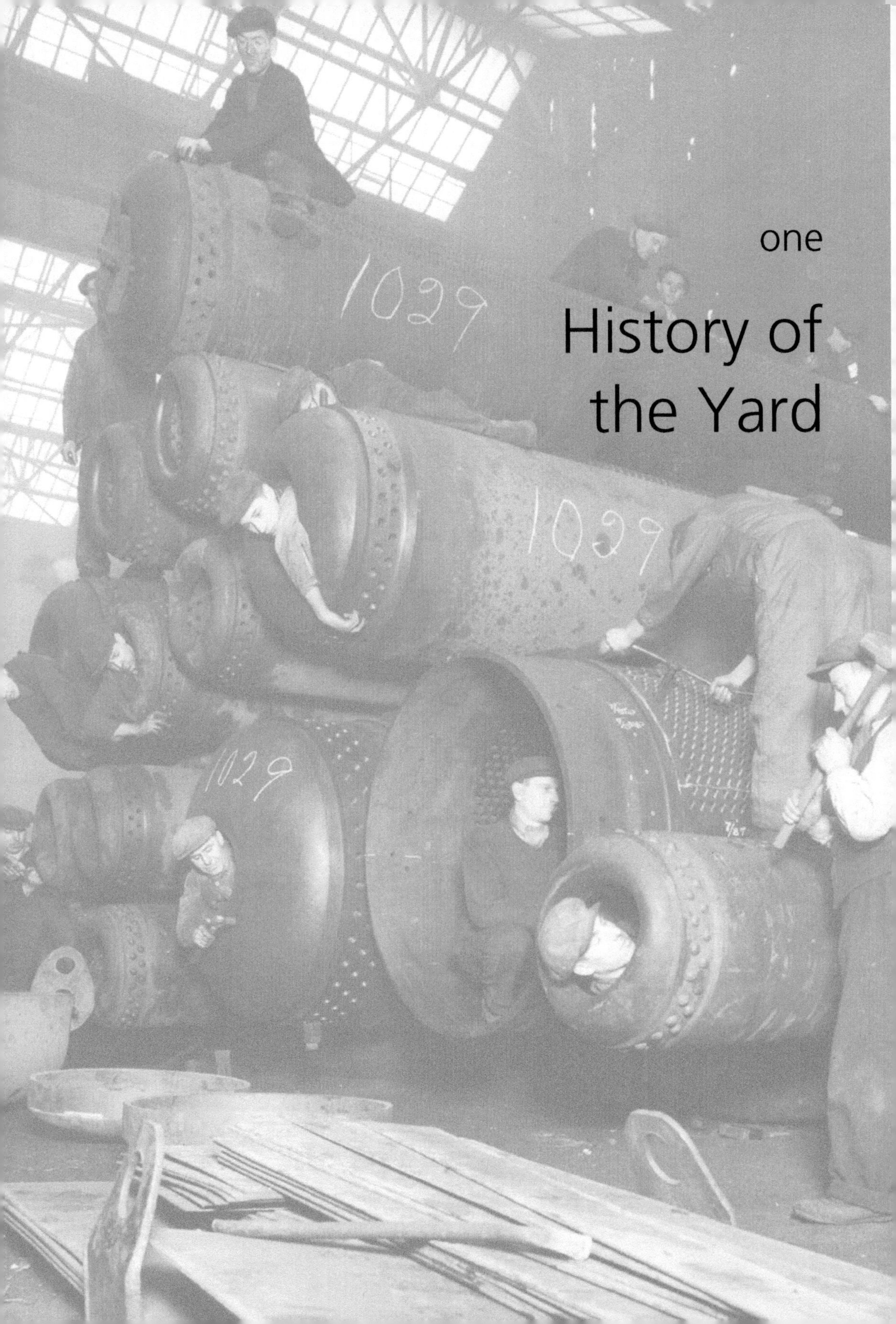
one

History of
the Yard

Above: *The yard in the 1850s. (Courtesy of Wirral Archives Service)*

Right: *John Laird. (Courtesy of Wirral Archives Service)*

William Laird came to Liverpool in 1810 to build up orders for his father's rope works in Greenock. He was thirty years of age and when he failed to achieve the amount of orders he had anticipated, he became director of two shipping companies, set up an agency for James Watt's steam engine and purchased a sugar house.

While Liverpool was developing and prospering during the Industrial Revolution, Birkenhead was suffering from a lack of investment in its potential. Laird started to buy land on the Birkenhead side of the Mersey with the intention of building harbour facilities and a canal across the Wirral Peninsular. The plan was to sail ships up the river Dee and cross to Birkenhead on the canal.

His first land purchase was on the north side of Wallasey Pool where there was a wooden jetty named Vittoria Wharf. He built a boiler works there that became the Birkenhead Iron Works. Laird alone could not finance the programme and he made attempts to sell the scheme to potential partners and investors.

Although his plans for a port to compete with Liverpool failed to materialise through lack of capital, he went ahead to develop a town for the workers. The town was centred on Hamilton Square, named after an ancestor who became an Archbishop in Scotland. He built his own house in Cathcart Street and, in 1828 the Birkenhead Iron Works received its first order to build a ship. William Laird's son, John, who was a trained solicitor, also joined the company in 1828.

The Irish Inland Steam Navigation Co. ordered a 90ft iron lighter that was completed in 1829 as the *Wye*. It was then taken to pieces and the sections were taken to Ireland and reassembled. The owners were so pleased with the vessel that they placed an order for two further lighters and, in 1830 ordered a 113ft-long paddle steamer that was equipped with watertight bulkheads and named *Lady Lansdowne*.

In the 1830s, William and John Laird made the decision that the way forward in the construction of ships was that they should be built of iron and not wood. In 1837 they invited Professor Airey, the Astronomer Royal, to carry out tests on board the latest ship, the *Rainbow*. He concluded that the mass of iron on an iron vessel took the compass off course but that it was possible to make allowances to correct the readings.

The *John Randolph*, the first iron ship to be built for a North American ship-owner, was completed in 1834, and the *Rainbow*, the largest ever iron ship, was handed over to the General Steam Navigation Co. in 1837. Also in 1837, John Ericsson launched an experimental screw vessel and named it *Francis B. Ogden*. However, when he tried to sell the design to the Admiralty, they declined his offer. At the time, Lt Robert F. Stockton USN was in England looking for financial backing for the Delaware and Raritan Canal in New Jersey, which was owned by his family.

Stockton commissioned Ericsson to build a similar screw propeller vessel which was powered by a two-cylinder, direct acting steam engine driving a twin screw inside a hollow outer shaft, mounting another screw which turned in the opposite direction. Ericsson, who later altered it by removing one of the screws, held the patent for this design. The vessel was launched in 1838 and named *Robert F. Stockton*.

When the ship was sent on trials it achieved 4½ knots towing a 650-ton ship against a 2-knot current. The ship was rigged as a schooner and sailed to New York in 1839. She was renamed *New Jersey* the following year and gave excellent service to the Delaware and Raritan Canal Co., working on the canal until she was scrapped in 1871. The British Patent Office made an unsuccessful attempt to purchase the ship's machinery to place alongside *Comet*.

The Rainbow *was built in 1837 for the General Steam Navigation Co. (Courtesy of Wirral Archives Service)*

The Robert F. Stockton *was built in 1838 and was Lairds first screw-driven ship. (Courtesy of Wirral Archives Service)*

Nemesis was the first iron ship to round the Cape of Good Hope. (Courtesy of Wirral Archives Service)

The yard had assisted the East India Co. to explore the sea route to India when the Lairds-built *Euphrates* took travellers from the Persian Gulf to India. *L'Egyptien*, also built at Birkenhead, was the first iron vessel to make the passage from Britain to Alexandria and up the river Nile. Seventeen new ships had been built at the yard by 1838 but owners were still sceptical of the benefits of iron ships and it became difficult to obtain orders for the yard.

Nemesis was ordered by the East India Co. for service in China and was completed in 1839. Her shallow draft of 6ft made her an ideal vessel to navigate up rivers and she had the ability to sail to windward. On her maiden voyage she ran aground off St Ives in Cornwall, as her compass correctors had not been fitted correctly. However, very little damage occurred and she was soon refloated.

In 1840 she sailed to India and was the first iron ship to round the Cape of Good Hope, and was forced into Delagoa Bay after beaching on the South African coast. She arrived at the Bogue Forts in China in November that year to be involved in the fighting in the First Opium War. As she experienced less damage than the wooden ships she was instrumental in the Royal Navy adding more iron ships to the fleet.

Nemesis returned to Bombay for repairs and then saw service between Bombay, Karachi and Bassein. She was involved in an attack on pirates at Malloodoo Bay in September 1845. She was ordered from Hong Kong to Rangoon in July 1852 and continued service in the China Seas for several months until she was sold later that year.

The first iron-built ship for the British Government was constructed in 1840. She was a 113ft packet named *Dover* and was followed by an order for four gunboats for the Royal Navy and John Laird decided to build a frigate that was propelled by paddle wheels.

A change of policy by the Admiralty in the 1840s resulted in the placing of an order for five iron frigates. One of these was given to Lairds to construct and she was the first of the class to be launched as the *Birkenhead*. She was later converted to a troop-ship but, on a voyage from Cork to South East Africa struck a submerged rock off the Cape of Good Hope and sank.

Guadeloupe was the world's largest iron ship when she was built in 1842 and was designed at the yard with the intention of selling her to the Royal Navy. However, when the navy decided that they were not interested in iron warships, she was purchased by the Mexican Navy and commanded by Capt. Edward Philip Charlwood, who was a Royal Navy captain and able to provide the Royal Navy with first-hand knowledge of how iron vessels handled in various conditions. The gun platform on *Guadeloupe* was steadier than on older ships and when there was a direct hit to the vessel the deck or hull did not splinter, which was one of the main causes of fatalities on the traditional wooden-built ships.

Prince Ernest was built in 1846; in 1854 she was taken over by the South Eastern Railway and was lengthened in 1861 during an overhaul at Folkestone. On 31 August that year she was the first ship to sail from a new pier in Folkestone and in 1865 she carried out a programme of day excursions from that port. In 1870 she had new boilers installed and was broken up in 1886.

Cambria was built at the yard as the largest of four sister ships ordered for the Holyhead to Kingstown service. The *Scotia*, *Anglia* and *Hibernia* were completed in 1847 and *Cambria* followed a year later. A Parliament Act was passed in 1848 which enabled the railway company to own and operate their own ships. *Scotia* sailed on the first sailing for the company on 1 August that year.

All four vessels were taken over by the London & North Western Railway Co. in 1859 and in 1861 the terminal was transferred to Dublin's North Wall. *Scotia* and *Anglia* were sold and acted as blockade runners for the Confederate States during the American Civil War, based at Bermuda. Both vessels were captured at sea in October 1862. *Scotia* was renamed *General Banks* in 1863 and sold, while *Anglia* was renamed *Fanny & Jane* in 1865, following a grounding and subsequent salvage.

Lairds built the Ma Robert *for Doctor Livingstone in 1858. (Courtesy of Wirral Archives Service)*

Connaught *was built in 1860 for the City of Dublin Steam Packet Co. (Courtesy of Wirral Archives Service)*

Hibernia was lengthened in 1861 and after she was sold to the Limerick & Waterford Railway Co. in 1877, she remained at Waterford until 1897 when she was sold to a scrap dealer at Bristol. She sank off the Smalls while being towed to Bristol. *Cambria* was also lengthened in 1861, re-boilered in 1866, and survived until 1884 when she was sold to the shipbreakers.

In 1852 John Lairds built *Forerunner* along with two similar sisters, *Faith* and *Hope*, for the African Steamship Co.'s services from London and Plymouth. *Forerunner* was launched on 3 July and was painted with a white hull for the Plymouth to Madeira, Tenerife, Bathurst and Freetown service. *Faith*'s completion was delayed and compensation was paid by the yard as tonnage had to be chartered to replace her. In her first year of service *Forerunner* experienced heavy weather in the Bay of Biscay and she was de-masted and then repaired at Gibraltar. Only two years later she was wrecked on the Isle of Fora at Madeira when fourteen people were lost and an Inquiry found the master to have been negligent.

Faith was placed on the London, Plymouth to West Africa service but in her first year of service an air pump failed and the vessel was forced to return to Falmouth. In 1854 she was chartered to the Admiralty for service in the Crimean War and the following year she was sold to the Government of Turkey but sank off the Isle of Wight on the voyage to Constantinople.

Hope, the third sister, was also delivered late and further compensation had to be paid by John Laird. She was also chartered for Crimean War service and returned to the West Africa route in 1855. She was laid up in 1856 and sold to James Moss of Liverpool in 1860. She was lengthened in 1864 and became *Luxor*, then in 1877 she was sold to H.Clapham of Newcastle. She gave service until 1898, when she was broken up at Walker on Tyne.

Charity was launched in 1853 for the African Steam Ship Co., and was sold to the Canadian Steam Navigation Co. of Liverpool in 1853 for the Liverpool to Quebec service. She was then chartered as a troop-ship during the Crimean War. At the end of the war she was sold to Linea de Vapores Correos Espanoles Transatlanticos at Cadiz and renamed

Alabama was built in 1862 for the Confederates in the American Civil War. (Courtesy of Wirral Archives Service)

Cubana for their Cadiz to Havana service. In 1864 she was bought by Lamport & Holt, and became *Herschel*, sailing from Liverpool to Pernambuco, Bahia, Rio de Janeiro, Montevideo and Buenos Aires.

In 1872 she was sold again, to Robert Sloman of Hamburg, and renamed *Palmerston*. She was converted to a four-masted sailing ship and sailed in their fleet until 1890, when she was sold to Bruckner & Albers of Hamburg. She was renamed *Federico* in 1894 and broken up at Genoa in 1899.

In the 1840s many people felt that the yard would close because of the lack of orders for new vessels. However, the scrapping of the Navigation Laws that were designed to protect British merchant ships from foreign competition, meant that owners needed to look at replacing many of their older vessels. Also, Lloyds finally acknowledged the existence of the iron ship in 1856 by publishing regulations governing the specifications of these vessels.

An Act of Parliament was passed in 1856 regarding the lack of progress on the completion of Birkenhead docks. The Mersey Docks & Harbour Board was established in 1858, with the appointment of John Laird as a nominee of the government. A new site on the riverbank was acquired between Monks Ferry and Tranmere Pool, as the Wallasey Pool yard was needed as part of the new dock system.

It was during this period that the yard's reputation was established and new orders came from various shipping lines. The passenger liners *Nubia* and *Pera* were built for the P&O Line and cross-channel steamers constructed for the Irish Sea and English Channel routes. In 1860, the Institution of Naval Architects was created. Macgregor Laird made several trips to Africa and a settlement called Lairdstown was founded. The yard was visited by Dr Livingstone, who placed an order for a river steamer that was named *Ma Robert*, after his wife. Macgregor also founded the African Steam Navigation Co., which was later taken over by Elder Dempster & Co.

Although the orders for merchant vessels were progressing during this time the Admiralty were still reluctant to place orders for iron-built ships. Lairds had built four gunboats for the East India Co. in 1839 that had been sent to China to support the naval vessels in the war against opium smuggling.

Birkenhead became the first town to adopt a system of horse-drawn tramcars in 1860 and its population had increased to just under 40,000. In 1860, William Laird designed three ships for the City of Dublin Steam Packet Co.: the *Ulster*, *Munster* and *Connaught*. Twenty years later, the Post Office invited tenders for an improved mail service to Ireland and the three vessels were re-engined by Lairds, giving them an extra 2 knots of speed. Several years later, the yard built four vessels for the Irish trade that were twin-screwed and were capable of a speed of 23 knots. *Ulster*, *Munster*, *Connaught* and *Leinster* were launched in 1896.

In 1863, the yard built the *Alabama* for the Confederates in the American Civil War. Numerous attempts were made to prevent her delivery so it was arranged that she did not return to the yard after her trails. The Lairds staff and guests were taken ashore off the Welsh coast and she sailed to the Azores, where she was handed over to her new crew.

John Laird retired in 1861 and became the first Member of Parliament for the town in 1863. While out riding with his daughter in 1874, he was involved in an accident and died. The control of the yard had already passed to his sons, William, John and Henry. William had joined the firm after he left school at Harrow and became a trained ship designer. John served a commercial apprenticeship with a firm of Brazilian merchants and Henry was trained in the drawing office of a French shipbuilder. At the Birkenhead yard he took over the drawing office. The yard consisted of five graving docks, two of which were over 400ft long, and four building slipways.

HMS *Captain* was a masted turret ship, launched on 27 March 1869 by Cammell Laird. She was designed by Capt. Cowper Phipps Coles, who was responsible for designing the gun turrets that were fitted to most turret ships of the late nineteenth century. Following the launch, it was discovered that the ship was 735 tons heavier than the design because Coles had suffered an illness during the construction and was unable to supervise the work.

She was armed with two turrets, each containing twin 25-ton muzzle loading rifled guns firing 600-pound shells, and was armoured with 7/8in plates along the hull, 12in over turrets, and the armour had a 12in teak backing. The ship was propelled by coal-fired steam engines that gave a service speed of 14 knots. As the heavily armoured turrets tended to make the ship unstable, it was important to reduce the freeboard which brought these weights close to the centre of gravity but made them vulnerable to flooding in bad weather. The designed freeboard was 8ft, which minimised the amount of hull exposed to enemy fire, but the additional weight brought this down to 6ft 6in.

HMS *Captain* was commissioned on 30 April 1870. On 6 September that year she was sailing off Cape Finisterre with a convoy of ten other ships when she started to heel over. Her draft and rigid masting gave her a maximum stability of only 21° against over 60° for most other navy ships. The captain immediately ordered that the topsail be cut away, but before this could be completed she capsized, with a loss of 480 lives. Only eighteen members of the crew were saved. An investigation concluded that the vessel was not stable and that: 'the *Captain* was built in deference to public opinion expressed in Parliament and through other channels'.

Santa Rosa was built by the yard in 1872 for the Pacific Steam Navigation Co.'s service from Liverpool to Valparaiso and Calloa via the Panama Canal service. In 1890 she was sold to Lota Coal Co. and then to Cousino Cia, Valparaiso, and was renamed *Luis Cousino*. She was broken up in 1902.

Tacna was also built for the Pacific Steam Navigation Co. for their coastal services around the Pacific coast of South America. On 7 March 1874, she sailed from Valparaiso on a voyage to Port de Azucar, with general cargo and ten cattle on deck. As the weather deteriorated, she developed a list and then there was an explosion that blew a hole in the deck. *Tacna* sank and nineteen of the crew lost their lives. The captain was arrested by the Chilean authorities but was later released following negotiations by the British consul.

Rose and her sister *Shamrock* were built in 1875 and 1876 respectively, and operated Holyhead to Dublin on the express daylight sailings service. In 1887 *Rose* had new boilers fitted and, in 1893 on a voyage from Holyhead a crankshaft broke and the engine was badly damaged and she had to be towed back to North Wales. She was sent to Birkenhead to be surveyed by her builders and it was decided that the repairs were uneconomical to complete. *Rose* was sold to shipbreakers on the Mersey, and scrapped in 1896. *Shamrock* was replaced on the service in 1898 by a new vessel, but the following year she was also scrapped.

Barbary was built in 1877 and only served for four years with her original owner. She was sold to the Booth Steam Ship Co. in 1881, and retained the same name. She was renamed *Clement* in 1882 and was sold to Empreza Nav. Gram Para, becoming *Marajo* in 1897. In 1900 she was sold to Cia de Cabotagem do Grao Para and was broken up in 1913.

In 1877 a cross-channel vessel named *Isabella* and the first Cock tug, *Storm Cock*, were constructed and delivered by Lairds. *Theresinense* was a shallow draft paddle-steamer that was launched at Birkenhead on the 26 August 1880 for a service from Theresina to Maranham. In 1891 she was owned by Cia de Navegacao a Vapor do Rio Parnahyba and was sailing from Theresina. She was sold in 1906 and scrapped the following year. *Cephalonia* was built for the Cunard Line and was the largest ship built at Birkenhead when she was launched on 20 May 1882.

The vessel Birkenhead was the first of seven similar sisters and was launched as *Duke of Clarence* and completed in 1891 for the Fleetwood to Belfast service, operated jointly by the Lancashire & Yorkshire Railway Co. and the London & North Western Railway Co. In 1906 she was transferred to the Lancashire & Yorkshire Railway Co. and placed on the Hull to Zeebrugge summer service and the Liverpool to Drogheda winter route. In 1907 she was re-boilered during an overhaul at Birkenhead.

In 1914, at the outbreak of the First World War, she became an Armed Boarding Steamer in the Channel, and later in the Northern Patrol, resuming the Zeebrugge service in 1920. Transferred to the London & North Western Railway in 1922 and to the London Midland & Scottish Railway the following year, she was withdrawn and laid up at Fleetwood in 1929 and sold to Thos. W. Ward in 1930 and broken up at Barrow.

HMS *Rattlesnake* was designed as a torpedo boat catcher but was too slow in her role; in 1893 Lairds launched HMS *Ferret* and HMS *Lynx*, which were both torpedo boat destroyers, faster than *Rattlesnake* and easier to manoeuvre. By the end of the nineteenth century the yard had built nineteen of these vessels for the Royal Navy. In the last ten years of the nineteenth century Lairds built seventy-one ships, forty-six of these vessels being warships or naval auxiliaries.

City of Belfast was the first screw-operated vessel built for the Barrow Steam Navigation Co.'s Barrow to Belfast route, and was built at the yard in 1893. She was taken over by the Midland Railway in 1907 and, in the First World War she became HMS *City of Belfast* and operated as an armed boarding and inspection vessel. At the end of the war she was returned to her owners. In 1925 was sold to Constantine Togias of Greece and renamed *Nicolaos Togias*. She was scrapped in 1932.

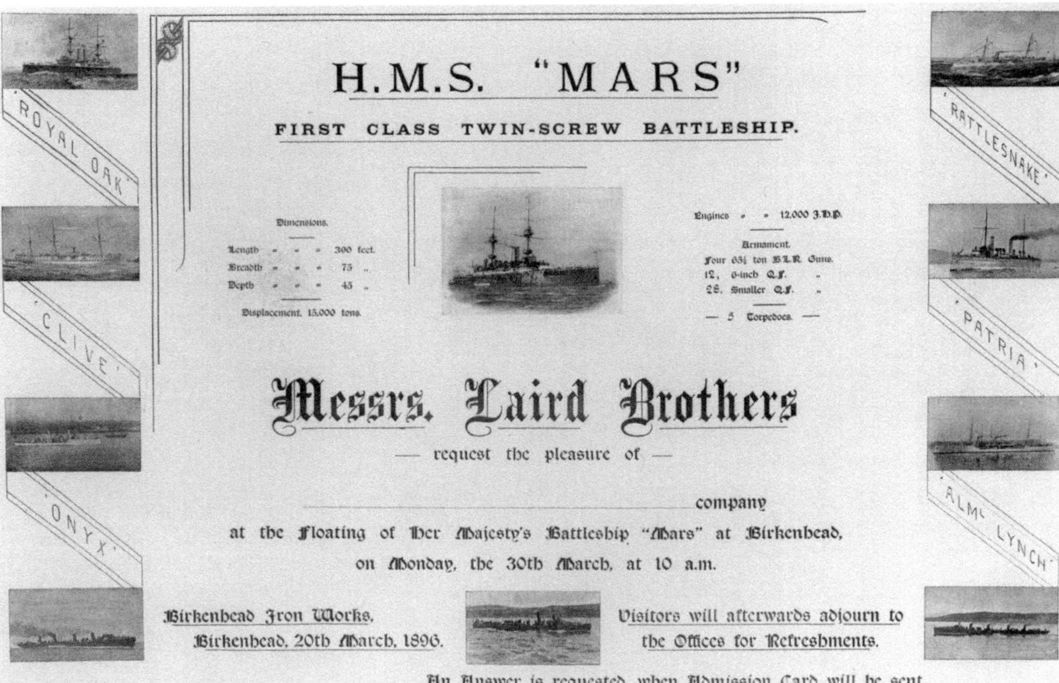

Above: *The launch ticket for the battleship HMS* Mars, *which was built in 1896. (Courtesy of Wirral Archives Service)*

Right: *Liverpool Screw Towing Co. advertisement showing* Black Cock *towing an Admiralty Floating Dock from Birkenhead to Portsmouth in 1912, and* Pea Cock *and* Flying Cock *towing the Admiralty Floating Dock.*

Presidente Sarmiento was ordered by the Argentine Government for sail training purposes and was named in 1898 after one the founders of the country's naval academy. She completed thirty-seven long distance voyages, including seven circumnavigations and trained more than 1,000 officers between 1898 and 1938. She also represented Argentina at coronations and presidential inaugurations in Spain, Chile, Mexico, Britain and the United States.

She carried two 4.7in, two 4in, and two 6in powder guns and also had three deck mounted torpedo tubes. Following the completion of her sail training duties, she was laid up in 1938 and served as a training ship until she was decommissioned in 1961. Since then she has been a museum ship at a permanent berth at Buenos Aires alongside the bark rigged hydrographic survey vessel *Uruguay* that was built as the *Parana* in 1874.

Between 1870 and 1900 the yard built 270 vessels, including liners for the Cunard Steamship Co., Inman's International Line and sixteen vessels for the Pacific Steam Navigation Co. The steam yacht *Valiant* was constructed for the American millionaire W.K. Vanderbilt. Between 1885 and 1900, HMS *Royal Oak*, HMS *Mars*, HMS *Glory* and HMS *Exmouth* were delivered to the Royal Navy.

It became clear during this period that Lairds were becoming increasingly un-successful in tendering for large cargo vessels and passenger liners. The largest dry dock was only 440ft long and it was apparent that an ambitious programme of expansion and reconstruction was required to enable the yard to compete with the other major United Kingdom shipbuilders.

In 1900, Laird Brothers and John Jones & Sons formed the Tranmere Bay Development Co. and a programme of expansion was instituted: the total area of the yard was increased to 98½ acres; the 15-acre fitting-out basin was the largest private wet dock in Britain; six new slipways were laid down, with the longest able to accommodate a vessel 1,000ft long. Two new dry docks were built, engine and repair ships completed and linked to a new rail system and heavy capacity cranes built.

William, John and Henry Laird had died before the turn of the century and their places were taken by their sons, J. Macgregor Laird, Roy M. Laird and J.W.P. Laird. A public company was formed in 1900, which became Laird Brothers & Co. Ltd. Mr R.R. Bevis, the Engineering Manager until his retirement, became the fourth director, and his son Ratsey Bevis was appointed Engineering Manager.

At this time the Admiralty decided that it was preferable for one contractor to be totally responsible for the complete construction of naval vessels. Vickers merged with Maxim, Armstrong & Whitworth and the Sheffield firm of Charles Cammell joined with Lairds in 1903. The firm was founded in 1828 by Charles Cammell to produce rails, switches, carriage wheels and other railway equipment. By 1861 it was producing armour plating, which Lairds used in the building of naval vessels.

Cammell part owned an ordnance works at Coventry, coal mines, iron ore mines and smelting works at Workington and a file factory at Odessa in Russia. It had a steel and iron works at Penistone and two steel works in Sheffield. The merged concern was named Cammell Laird and Co. Ltd with J. MacGregor Laird as its chairman.

The Mersey Docks & Harbour Board placed an order for an 8,590-ton sand pump dredger in 1908, which was named *Leviathan*. She was 148m by 21m and the dredging machinery consisted of four centrifugal pumps driven by four sets of inverted triple expansion engines. These were connected to four suction tubes 27m long and 1.25m in internal diameter. The following year the 7,117-ton passenger and chilled meat vessel *Highland Laddie* was launched for the Nelson Steam Navigation Co.

Snowdrop was built in 1910 for the Seacombe, Egremont and New Brighton to Liverpool

The Cunard Liner Campania *(1893/12,950grt) was built by the Fairfield Ship Building Co. at Glasgow and in November, 1914 she was chartered by the Admiralty and converted into an Armed Merchant Cruiser by Cammell Laird. A flight platform was installed forward and she was also fitted with 8 x 4.7in guns. Her foremast was removed and a slope fitted with a hanger on the top of the bridge. (Courtesy of Wirral Archives Service)*

ferry service operated by the Borough of Wallasey. She operated on these services until she was sold to the London & North Eastern Railway in 1936 when her superstructure was altered and she was converted to carry vehicles. In 1937 she was renamed *Thane of Fife* and operated on the Granton to Burtisland ferry service. Mrs A.D.G. Speevack purchased her in 1948 to operate excursions in the Granton area and she survived until 1953 when she was broken up.

In 1910 William Lionel Hichens replaced Dr Francis Elgar who had been chairman of the company since 1908. Mr R.R. Bevis retired as Managing Director and Mr J.G. Carter took over. The yard completed the largest floating dock in the world for the Admiralty in 1912. It was 640ft long and designed to lift vessels up to 32,000 tons. Two 9,000-ton passenger-cargo liners were ordered by P&O which were named *Khiva* and *Khyber* and two 10,625 liners *Bergensfjord* and *Kristianiafjord* were built for the Den Norske America Line.

Doon was launched on 22 January 1913 for the Royal Mail Steam Packet Co. She was a coastal vessel based at Buenos Aires with two other sisters and held Argentine registry although she was owned by a British company. By 1919 she was trading between European and British ports and, later that year she was sold to the Las Palmas Produce Co. and renamed *Britanica*.

In 1923 she was sold to the Anglo-South American Meat Co. of Argentina and the following year she was bought by the Union Cold Storage Co. with the Blue Star Line as managers. Early in the Second World War she was used as a store-ship at Scapa Flow and,

Above left and right: *The Cunard liner* Mauretania *under construction at the yard in 1938. (Courtesy of Wirral Archives Service)*

in 1946 she was moved to Singapore to act in a similar role. However, the venture did not prove successful and she was laid up and brought back to London's Royal Victoria Dock in 1947, where she was again laid up. The following year she was sold to a Belgium company and converted to a barge to transport scrap metal between Antwerp and Willebroek. She was later broken up in Belgium.

The *King Orry* was launched for the Isle of Man Steam Packet Co. on 11 March 1913 and the yard's first train ferry, *Leonard*, was launched for the Canada Trans-Continental Railway. She was built for service in the St Lawrence and was later sold to Shell and converted to an oil tanker. Work on an experimental submarine was started prior to the First World War and a prototype, the *E41*, was completed in 1915. A further seven submarines were built at the yard during the war. The cruisers HMS *Chester* and HMS *Swift* were also completed for service in the war.

Experimental work on boilers took place at this time, following a serious accident on HMS *Dartmouth* in 1915 when the wrapper plate blew off one of the water drums and scalded nineteen men to death in the stokehold. The Admiralty commissioned Cammell Laird to attempt to solve the problem of higher performances demanded by warfare on boilers in warships. The chief draftsman devised a new type of boiler that was fitted to over fifty warships, and other shipyards were instructed by the Admiralty to adopt the new design.

Submarine E41 was commissioned in 1915 and the class was the backbone of the submarine service in the First World War. They were the first submarines converted to carry mines and Cammell Laird also built E42, E45 and E46. Each submarine was crewed by three officers and twenty-eight ratings. E41 served with the 8th Flotilla and was based at Harwich during the war. Six of the submarines were classed as minelayers and carried twenty mines. At the end of the war eleven were at Harwich, six in the Tees, two at Killybegs, six in the Mediterranean and four were based in the Adriatic. E41 was sold in 1922.

During the First World War the yard completed work on 9 battleships, 60 cruisers, 100 British and 95 United States destroyers, 8 submarines, 123 armed merchant vessels and 107 merchant ships. The Cunard passenger liner *Campania* and the Isle of Man Steam Packet Co. steamer *Ben-My-Chree* were converted to the first seaplane carriers to work with the Royal Navy.

Stavangerfjord was completed by Cammell Laird in 1918 and sailed to New York on 29 April that year, then was laid up until she sailed on her maiden voyage from New York to Oslo on 11 September. During her refit in 1924, she was converted to oil burning and at a refit at Bremen in 1931 she was fitted with low-pressure turbines.

At the outbreak of the Second World War she was laid up at Oslo and, when the Germans occupied the country, she was used as an accommodation ship for the German navy. Her first post-war sailing was in August 1945, when she sailed from Oslo to New York. Another major overhaul and refit occurred in 1956 when her tonnage was increased to 14,015grt. On 4 February 1964, she arrived at Hong Kong to be broken up. She had completed over 800 Atlantic voyages, steamed more than 5,000,000 miles and carried over 410,000 passengers.

Following the end of the war there was a boom in shipbuilding and the yard was very busy, productive and profitable. In 1919 British shipyards produced 1,620,442 tons of new ships and the following year this rose to 2,055,624 tons. However, by 1921 this had dropped to 1,538,052 tons because of a reduction in freight cargo rates. Also, a disarmament conference in 1921 called for a ten-year break from new naval building and the Admiralty suspended work on four capital ships and all other construction.

However, the yard was given permission to complete the construction of HMS *Rodney* and managed to obtain orders for a number of merchant vessels, including the 17,750 ton passenger liner, *De Grasse*, for La Compagnie Generale Transatlantique. In 1920 the first ever all welded vessel, *Fullagar*, was completed for the Anchor Brocklebank Line.

In 1922, following the death of Sir George J. Carter, the company appointed Robert Stewart Johnson as Managing Director. He was responsible for authorising an extensive modernisation programme in the yard in the 1920s and for assembling a team to devise plans for the future prosperity of the yard. Mr William McMenemy was the Engineering Manager, Mr J. Hamilton the Shipbuilding Manager and Mr James Morton was also part of the management team.

At the beginning of the 1930s, foreign governments started to offer subsidies to their shipbuilders and ship-owners which enabled them to build vessels at prices that British yards could not compete with. In 1931 there was only one ship on the order book and the workforce had been reduced to 2,000. HMS *Achilles* was built in 1933 and was a cruiser which, together with HMS *Exeter* and HMS *Ajax*, damaged the German pocket battleship, *Admiral Graf Spee*, in the Battle of the river Plate on 13 December, 1939. After the war she was recommissioned into the new Royal New Zealand Navy and, in 1948 became RIN *Delhi* in the Royal Indian Navy.

The tide did not turn for the yard until 1935 when the Admiralty placed an order for the first vessel to be designed and built as an aircraft carrier. She was launched by Lady Hoare in 1937, who named her *Ark Royal*. She cost over £3 million and became the largest ship yet to be constructed by the yard. The launch was watched by over 30,000 people.

City of Edinburgh was the first vessel to be built for Ellerman's City Lines by Cammell Laird and, following delivery in 1938, she was placed on their service from America to Australia and New Zealand. In 1941 she suffered a fire while berthed at Takordai and was towed out to sea, as there was a danger that she would block the port if the fire caused her to capsize. However, the fire was brought under control and the ship was saved.

In 1943 she was requisitioned by the Admiralty and converted into a Landing Ship Headquarters at Liverpool. She was fitted with two twin 4in guns, six sets of Oerlikon AA guns and six landing craft, becoming HMS *Lothian*. She joined the United States 7th Fleet and, in August 1944 she sailed from the Clyde to the Pacific via New York and Panama. There were 750 servicemen on board against the ship's capacity of 450 and, on 1 September when she berthed at Balboa, an armed mutiny took place on board. The Royal Marines were used to restore order and the men involved had their sentences suspended because there were no prison facilities available.

She arrived at Langemack Bay at New Guinea on 29 September and was ordered to join the Philippines Invasion Fleet. After spending some time in the Philippines, she sailed to Australia and docked at Sydney, where she arrived on 23 February, 1945. At Sydney, she was appointed as flagship to Rear Admiral Fleet Train D.B. Fisher CB, CBE, ADC. Following duties in Australian waters, she was sent to Singapore, Hong Kong and Shanghai and was used to evacuate British civilians and prisoners of war.

Early in 1946 she sailed back to Britain via India and, following decommissioning, was returned to Ellerman City Lines on the Mersey in April that year. She received an extensive overhaul and was converted to her original form in 1947, then was allocated to the Ellerman & Bucknall fleet. *City of Edinburgh* survived until 1961, when she was sold for breaking up and renamed *Castle Mount* for the delivery voyage to Hong Kong.

Following the launch of *Ark Royal*, work commenced on the Cunard liner *Mauretania*, on the same slipway, and work was progressing on the battleship HMS *Prince of Wales*. Work was carried out to re-engine and re-boiler HMS *Renown*, in which four sets of machinery were built and eight water tube boilers were constructed. These were shipped to Portsmouth Dockyard, where they were installed in the battle cruiser.

In the Second World War, the yard completed repairs on 120 warships, including 9 battleships and 11 aircraft carriers, and 2,000 merchant vessels. They built 106 naval vessels, averaging one ship delivered every twenty days. They also completed 13 other vessels during the war.

Robert Johnson was appointed chairman of the company in 1940 and was knighted in 1942. He was responsible for changing production from naval to merchant vessels at the end of hostilities. The major British shipping lines had lost many of their vessels during the war and each was embarking on dramatic replacement programmes. The passenger and cargo liners *Corinthic* and *Ceramic* were built for Shaw Savill and Albion Line and the refrigerated cargo vessel *Persic* was also handed over to the same company.

King Orry, *Tynwald*, and *Snaefell* were delivered to the Isle of Man Steam Packet Co. and the *St Patrick* and *St David* to the Great Western Railway. New ships were delivered to Ellerman Lines and passenger and cargo vessels were built for the Blue Star Lines services to South America. The Liverpool-based Blue Funnel Line, the British & Continental Line and the Booth Steamship Co. also ordered vessels from the yard. Oil tankers were built for the Anglo-Saxon Petroleum Co., the British Tanker Co., Athel Line, Esso Petroleum Co. and the Burmah Oil Co.

On 28 August 1951, the chairman Robert Johnson died and was succeeded by Mr J.C. Mather. His son, Robert White Johnson, was appointed as Managing Director. In 1954 the yard became Cammell Laird & Co.(Shipbuilders and Engineers) and continued to rationalise and modernise under the new chairman.

The second *Ark Royal* was handed over to the Royal Navy in 1955. She had been launched by the Queen Mother on 3 May 1950 and incorporated all the modern technological advances that were required by the Royal Navy.

In 1957 the company announced a reconstruction programme that involved building large prefabricated units in new shipbuilding shops. The giant units would be lifted by 100-ton cranes, onto the adjoining slipways. Plans were also announced to construct a new dry dock to accommodate the large tankers that were being ordered by many of the oil companies. The dry dock is 850ft long and 140ft wide and was part of the reconstruction programme which also included the provision of a tanker-cleaning installation with a deep water berth at Rock Ferry. This was required on the river following the International Convention for the Prevention of Pollution of the Sea by Oil in 1954, and the Oil in Navigable Waters Act in 1955.

On 23 June 1959 the Queen Mother came to Birkenhead to launch the new Union Castle passenger vessel, *Windsor Castle*. She was the largest passenger ship built in Britain since the Second World War and the largest to be built in an English shipyard. HMS *Devonshire*, Britain's first ever gas turbine-powered guided missile ship was also in the course of construction in the yard at this time.

Princess Alexandra opened the new Princess dry dock in 1962, which was the largest privately owned dry dock in Britain. The dry dock was built on the site of the old No.5 dry dock and land was purchased by the company for this modernisation and improvement project, including part of Birkenhead Priory and St Mary's graveyard. It is 290m long with a 43m entrance. Quays on both sides have rail tracks connected to the yard's system, together with tracks for portal cranes. 15-ton cranes were provided and, on the south side there is a further crane capable of lifting 50 tons at 30m radius and 6 tons at 50m radius. The dock has a sliding caisson at the entrance that is operated by a large double-drum electric winch mounted on the gate itself.

In the early 1960s the chairman, R.W. Johnson, said that British shipbuilders were passing through difficult times with new orders few and far between. He felt strongly that shipyards needed to look increasingly towards modernisation and rationalisation. Modernisation was only part of the answer to meet the highly competitive conditions that existed at the time. He said that to survive, a shipyard needed to be ready to modernise its ideas and must have something new to offer in the way of ship design.

Her Majesty Queen Elizabeth the Queen Mother launches the Windsor Castle *on 23 June 1959.*

A view of the yard and fitting-out basin in 1959.

The shipbuilder needed be able to offer the most economic ship for a specific trade at the lowest price consistent with quality and, equally important, must be prepared to go out and sell their ships to the world. He said that Cammell Laird had consistently led in modernisation involving large-scale investment and in the introduction of new techniques and designs. One of the significant moves by the company at this time was to introduce their 'Selected Six' standard ships, including three dry cargo ships, two bulk carriers and a tanker.

Cammell Laird experts had been working on the designs and looked at the types and sizes of ships that it was felt were likely to be needed at the time. An important factor in the design of the ships was the attempt to keep the ships at a cost that was as low as possible, bearing in mind the need for maximum efficiency, economy and reliability.

The 'Selected Six' included:

1. A general cargo shelter deck motorship of 3,150/4,000 tons deadweight, with a length of 92m with everything aft, a total grain capacity of about 223,000 cu.ft or a bale capacity of about 203,000 cu.ft and a speed of 14¼ knots.

2. A larger vessel of 8,500/9,500 tons with a length of 125m, a total grain capacity of 530,000 cu.ft or a bale capacity of 490,000 cu.ft and, in the case of the first, her superstructure would be positioned aft and she would have a speed of 15¾ knots.

3. A motor cargo ship with a tonnage of around 10,500/12,500 deadweight tons, with a length of 135m and four forward holds, and one aft of the superstructure. She would have a total grain capacity of 655,000 cu.ft or a bale capacity of 608,000 cu.ft, with a speed of 14½ knots.

4. A 165m-long bulk carrier with a deadweight of 23,000 tons, with everything aft and a grain capacity of 1,190,000 cu.ft, and a speed of 15 knots.

5. A larger bulk carrier with a deadweight of 56,000 tons and a length of 230m, and a total grain capacity of 3,050,000 cu.ft, with a speed of 17 knots.

6. A tanker of 53,500/57,400 deadweight tons, a length of 230m and an oil capacity of about 2,495,000 cu.ft with all superstructure aft and a speed of 17 knots.

Standardisation in shipbuilding was not a new idea. In 1957 the yard launched the Shell tanker, *Hemifusus*, and details of Cammell Laird's expansion programme were announced. Shell Tankers suggested that consideration be given by shipbuilders and ship-owners to standardisation to a high degree that would not only lower prices but also bring faster building times. Shell felt that tankers were relatively uncomplicated compared with passenger liners and refrigerated cargo ships and that there was remarkable uniformity in the thinking of oil companies.

The *Hemifusus* was an 18,000-ton deadweight general purpose tanker designed for product distribution and was one of several similar size and tonnage vessels being introduced at the time by the major oil companies. Each of these classes of vessels had to be separately designed, blueprinted and treated in every way as if they were thousands of tons apart instead of only a few feet in dimensions. Shell encouraged co-operation between the main oil companies on the same hull form and other design details that would create significant savings in cost and in construction time. Up to that time shipbuilders had not had to look for work, as it was very much a seller's market.

The economic conditions that prevailed at the time made it very difficult to obtain orders on which the yard could make a reasonable profit. Consequently, they were forced to select the work that they had a reasonable chance of obtaining and completing detailed evaluations of their competitors in each particular case. Ship-owners were learning to ask for credit, and as well as building an economically operable ship, the yard had to be

Far right:
Robert W. Johnson

Right: *J.C. Mather, J.P.*

STANDARDISATION IN SHIPBUILDING . . . .

CAMMELL LAIRD *have introduced a unique and revolutionary development in shipbuilding by the production of these six standard ship designs.*

Called **THE SELECTED SIX,** *they comprise three cargo ships, two bulk carriers and a tanker.*

THE SELECTED SIX *have been specially designed to assist shipowners combat the intense competitive conditions prevailing in world shipping today. They are designed to be produced at low capital cost without lowering the standard of workmanship and materials, and to operate at maximum efficiency with economy and reliability.*

✳ Full details available
on request to:-

CAMMELL LAIRD
& Co (Shipbuilders & Engineers) Ltd
BIRKENHEAD

Shipbuilders to the World

An advertisement for 'The Selected Six'.

The North Yard in 1964. It had not been used since the launching of the Blue Star line vessel, Fremantle Star, *in April 1960. The North Yard was reopened in 1964 for the building of an Oberon submarine, the* Ben-My-Chree *for the Isle of Man Steam Packet Co. and the* Spero *for Ellerman's Wilson Line.*

The largest ship of the Mobil Tanker fleet to be over-hauled at a British shipyard.
S.T.S. MOBIL ENTERPRISE, *51,300 tons deadweight, in The Princess Dock — the biggest privately owned dry dock in the United Kingdom — 950 ft long by 140 ft wide.*

CAMMELL LAIRD are able to offer Shipowners a speedy and efficient service carried out with economy and skill at one of the largest and most up-to-date shipbuilding and ship-repairing establishments in the world.

Facilities at CAMMELL LAIRD include seven dry docks ranging up to 950 ft long by 140 ft wide at the entrance. A wet basin covering fourteen acres is equipped with a 100 ton travelling crane and a 200 ton floating crane. A tanker cleaning installation, accessible at all states of the tide, has recently been built adjacent to the repair yards.

And now the long established firm of shiprepairers on the River Mersey, Grayson Rollo & Clover Docks Limited, has joined the CAMMELL LAIRD Group of Companies adding five dry docks of up to 800 ft by 120 ft to the existing facilities.

CAMMELL LAIRD

& Co (Shipbuilders & Engineers) **Ltd**

BIRKENHEAD

Shipbuilders to the World

Advertisment in The Motor Ship *in 1963.*

Liverpool Screw Towing Co. advertisement featuring the Lairds-built tugs Heath Cock *and* West Cock.

able to arrange suitable finance. The shipyard, therefore, must not only have shipbuilding and engineering experts on its staff, but must also have its own qualified financial specialists.

Prior to 1957, the commercial department was largely concerned with buying materials and services for the yard but, by 1963, it was a much larger department, also dealing with contracts and finance. The commercial department was also responsible for exploring and developing contracts with overseas sub-contractors, enabling the company to buy equipment in the cheapest market subject to the maintenance of standards of quality.

Between 1957 and 1960, the yard completed *Heath Cock*, *West Cock*, *Pea Cock*, *Flying Cock* and *Weather Cock* for the Liverpool Lighterage Co. for use on various towage duties on the Mersey. The cable-ships *Retriever* and *Mercury* were completed in 1962, and the new Mersey ferry *Overchurch* was delivered to Birkenhead Corporation. On 16 October 1962, Cammell Laird announced that their own board – and that of Grayson Rollo and Clover Docks – had agreed the terms of a merger, which would form one of the most formidable shipbuilding, repairing and dry dock combines in the country.

The Isle of Man Steam Packet's first passenger car-ferry, *Manx Maid*, was completed in 1962, and incorporated a series of ramps which enabled cars to be loaded and unloaded at Douglas, Isle of Man, at any state of the tide. A near sister, *Ben-My-Chree*, followed in 1966.

When the *British Ensign* was built for the B.P. Tanker Co. Ltd in 1964, she was the seventeenth vessel the yard had built for the company and was also the largest and longest merchant ship built at Birkenhead. In terms of carrying capacity, she was also the largest cargo vessel yet built in the

United Kingdom for British owners. She was followed in 1965 by the 64,584 d.w. tanker *British Captain*, which was built for the same owners.

The car-ferry *Spero* was delivered to Ellerman's Wilson Line in 1966, the *Ulster Queen* to the Belfast Steamship Co., the *Lion* to Burns & Laird in 1967, and the *Koningen Juliana* for the Harwich to Hook of Holland service in 1968.

A trio of cargo liners were built for the Cunard Steamship Co.'s United Kingdom to New York service between 1964 and 1966, and were named *Scythia*, *Samaria* and *Scotia*. In October 1964, Cammell Laird informed the Cunard Line that they were unable to tender for the new transatlantic liner planned by the line. They said that because of their full order book, they could not deliver the ship on time. The commitment was such that they could not commence work on the new ship until nearly a year later than the date necessary to meet Cunard's delivery requirements. The order book comprised the two Polaris submarines, one conventional submarine, a super tanker, a large bulk carrier, two ferries, three cargo ships and some conversion contracts.

In 1963 an order for two Polaris submarines had been placed by the government. The keel of *Renown* was laid in June 1964, and *Revenge* in May the following year. *Renown* was launched in September 1967 and *Revenge* the following year. The order was clearly a very valuable one for the company and one that was gained at a time when competition for orders was fierce and the yard's profits were suffering.

The Polaris contract enabled the yard to reorganise, rationalise and renew its facilities and infrastructure. By 1969 the yard employed 11,400 people and it was estimated that the increase to cover the Polaris contract amounted to 40 per cent. Specialist workers in areas such as weapons, welding and quality control were recruited to supplement the other trades employed at the yard. *Renown* was completed in November 1968 and *Revenge* in December the following year. The hunter/killer submarine, *Conqueror*, was launched on 28 August 1969, and handed over to the Admiralty in November 1972.

The Government announced a financial reconstruction of the company in 1970 and took a 50 per cent interest in Cammell Laird & Co. (Shipbuilders and Engineers) with the company then ceasing to be part of the Laird Group. By 1972 the name became Cammell Laird Shipbuilders Ltd.

The Silver Chemical Line's *Silver Osprey* and *Silver Eagle* were delivered in 1969 and 1970. The Canadian Pacific Steamship's cargo vessel, *CP Voyager*, was handed over in 1970 and *CP Trader* in 1972. The small coastal tankers, *Esso Mersey* and *Esso Clyde*, were delivered to the Esso Petroleum Co. in 1972 and a trio of cargo vessels, *Orbita*, *Orduna* and *Ortega*, were built for the Royal Mail Lines in 1972/73.

In 1977, the company was nationalised and became part of British Shipbuilders. A covered construction hall which was 145m long, 107m wide and 50m high, was completed in 1978, and the Admiralty placed an order for three Type 42 destroyers which were named HMS *Coventry*, HMS *Birmingham* and HMS *Liverpool*. The oil platform *Sovereign Explorer* was built in dry docks 6 and 7, and was handed over in 1983. However, in 1985 the yard was denationalised and became a subsidiary of Vickers Shipbuilding & Engineering Ltd. The last surface ship built at the yard was HMS *Campbeltown*.

At the beginning of the 1990s, the yard was building three conventional submarines for the Royal Navy. HMS *Unseen* was handed over in 1991, HMS *Ursula* in 1992 and HMS *Unicorn* became the last boat to be built at Birkenhead when she was completed in 1993. However, prior to the delivery of this vessel, a government defence review declared the three submarines surplus to requirements and they were laid up and advertised for sale and eventually sold to the Canadian Government.

The covered construction hall that was built in 1978.

The shipyards that had specialised and relied on warship orders faced a particular problem at this time. The collapse of the Soviet Union brought a significant reduction in the orders from the Admiralty as part of the 'peace dividend'. Cammell Laird decided to change its status to a mixed yard that enabled it to tender for commercial contracts and apply for European Union grants for aid. However, by 1993, Vickers decided that it would not be seeking orders for the Birkenhead yard and it was closed that year. The yard ceased trading as Cammell Laird on 30 July that year.

The crisis in British shipbuilding in the 1990s was caused partly by the fact that the Government privatised the yards but did not help or assist them to modernise, which was what was happening in other countries. Germany applied for European subsidies to modernise their shipbuilding facilities. Consequently, it now costs less per person to produce each vessel and the ships are built quicker with modern equipment. Consequently, Germany can now undercut British yards when tendering for new contracts.

In 1995, Spain built forty-seven ships but this increased to ninety-one in 2000. There has been an increase from 22.5 million gross tonnes produced worldwide in 1995 to 31.5 gross tonnes in 2000. The White Paper produced by the shipbuilding forum in 1998 described the United Kingdom shipbuilding industry as a 'small industrial sector consisting of eleven companies concentrating on niche markets for specialist and high value added ships, such as offshore oil exploration vessels, local ferries, dredgers and tugs'.

By 1995 new owners had reopened the yard under the Cammell Laird Group Holdings PLC name. They retained only one-third of the site and initially were tendering for repair and overhaul contracts. In 2000 the new Cammell Laird organisation employed 3,500 people worldwide and had yards in Britain, Gibraltar, Marseilles and Portland, Oregon. It reported pre-tax profits of £15.9 million in the financial year to April 2000 and claimed that was it receiving enquiries for business worth £750 million.

A contract to return to shipbuilding at the Birkenhead site was being discussed with a plan by Luxus (UK) Ltd to build two new luxury cruise ships worth £350 million. The contract was based on Luxus receiving government state aid and discussions with the relevant departments were in progress. The Department of Trade & Industry had offered £300 million in loan guarantees to cover the contract but was negotiating with the company to share another £100 million of risk.

The Company was also disappointed at the loss of an order, from the Ministry of Defence, for the construction of roll-on/roll-off ferries. Yards at Belfast, Glasgow and on the Tyne were awarded the contract and Cammell Laird claimed that they lost the contract

Edinburgh Castle *was purchased by Cammell Laird in 1999 and was sent to their yard on the Tyne for conversion and upgrading work.*

The yard in 2004.

The new section which was due to be fitted in Costa Classica *in 2000.*

because they had an almost full order book for its ship repair business, while failing yards had been rewarded.

In November 2000 the future of the yard was placed in jeopardy when a contract to install a new mid-section in an Italian liner was suspended. The contract with Costa Crociere was worth £51 million and involved inserting the new section into the liner between November 2000 and March 2001. Cammell Laird had agreed to a contract that stipulated that payment would be made on the completion of the work and had obtained credit to finance the project.

The *Costa Classica* was due to arrive at Birkenhead on the 23 November 2000 and the ship had left her homeport of Genoa with thirty Cammell Laird workers on board on 18 November. The following day, Costa recalled the vessel and the staff were put ashore at La Corunna in Spain. The direct and indirect impact of Costa's actions were very damaging to the company in the form of the loss of profit on the contract and significant cash flow problems.

Cammell Laird stated that they had also suffered the additional costs of downsizing the workforce, carrying excess overhead costs, and the significant negative impact on employee morale. They also felt that Costa's actions caused the trade and financial markets to have doubts about Cammell Laird's financial viability, which contributed to damaging the company's trading and financial position.

The main impact of the dispute with Costa created an environment of lower customer confidence and employee morale, leading to less work at tighter margins. The directors embarked on a strategy of reorganisation and a refocus of the business that included a financial restructuring and a possible sale of the company. When the Royal Bank of Scotland refused to extend an overdraft and payment facilities trading in Cammell Laird, shares were suspended on the Stock Exchange on 11 April 2001.

On 17 August 2001 the yard was bought for almost £10 million by the ship repair company, A&P. The chief executive of A&P said that there were not enough contracts to fill the two yards he already owned, let alone reopen Cammell Laird's Birkenhead, Teeside and Hebburn yards. The company was bought with finance from the Royal Bank Private Equity, the venture capital arm of the Royal Bank of Scotland, who owned 85 per cent of A&P.

The chief executive of A&P said that he did not have a goal for re-employment at any of the yards and that he could not promise that the yards would open up again. A&P had made a loss of £2 million the previous year and the company employed about 900 workers. However, orders for repair work and overhaul were obtained and the yard started work on various projects such as Irish Sea roll-on/roll-off ferries and coastal cargo vessels.

In July 2003 A&P announced the opening of A&P Tees, the former new Cammell Laird facility located on the mouth of the river Tees, near Middlesbrough. It was the last of the former Cammell Laird facilities taken over by the A&P Group to reopen following Hebburn and Birkenhead, which gave A&P facilities in virtually every major port throughout the country.

In January 2004 the A&P Group announced that it was considering breaking into the new building market at the old Cammell Laird site. It remains to be seen if shipbuilding will ever return to the banks of the Mersey but ship-repairing and conversion projects may continue at the yard as there are many Irish Sea vessels that require regular work. In the short period since A&P took over the yard they have attracted orders from most of the Irish Sea ferry and freight operators, for overhaul and minor conversion work. It is imperative, therefore, that A&P continue to remain competitive and the yard's good reputation may attract orders for work on merchant and naval vessels. This would enable the company to expand its operations at Birkenhead, making the future more secure for its workforce, and provide a welcome stimulation for the local economy on Merseyside.

In October 2004 it was announced that the A&P Group had sold its Birkenhead yard to the development company Reddington Finance. The sale included the leaseback of surplus land and A&P retained the ownership of the dry docks at the yard. Reddington acquired the other half of the former Cammell Laird site in 2003. A&P has assured the workforce that ship repair work will continue at the yard and said that they were on budget for 2004 by completing work on twenty-four ships by the middle of September.

*A&P Birkenhead
site plan.*

The Joiners
Shop in
2004.

At the beginning of 2007 it was announced that Peel Holdings PLC had bought the shipyard from Reddington Finance. It was hoped that this acquisition would ensure the future of the yard after Reddington had announced ambitious plans to redevelop the site. Peel stated that they saw the site as a valuable port facility, respecting its industrial heritage. The shipyard would continue to provide shiprepair and conversion facilities under the auspices of North Western Shiprepairers Limited, in which Peel had a major holding.

By May 2007, the company was employing over 500 people and was recognised as one of the major shiprepair and conversion companies in Europe. A contract was obtained in February 2008 to overhaul the Royal Fleet Auxilliary vessel *Fort Rosalie*. This was followed in June that year by an announcement that the company was successful in obtaining a £180 million contract from the Ministry of Defence to maintain and overhaul the Royal Fleet Auxiliary fleet of supply vessels. The contract could be extended for 25 years and the work may be worth up to £1 billion to the company.

A partnership deal was negiotiated later that year with the Italian shipbuilder Fincantieri to bid for six supply tankers for the Ministry of Defence. On the 17 November 2008, Northwestern Shiprepairers & Shipbuilders Limited was renamed Cammell Laird Shiprepairers & Shipbuilders Limited, when the company acquired the same name. Sales of more than £90.8 million were achieved for the year to May 2009, inccreasing its year on year sales by seventy per cent, with pre-tax profits increasing to £9.4 million. The success was attributed to the company's growing reputation for delivering a cost effective quality service.

In January 2010 Cammell Laird secured a contract worth £50 million to build the flight deck for the new aircraft carrier *Queen Elizabeth*. HMS *Queen Elizabeth* and HMS *Prince of Wales* are a two-ship class of aircraft carriers, which are being built to replace the *Invincible* class carriers. *Queen Elizabeth* is expected to enter service in 2016 and *Prince of Wales* will follow two years later.

Cammell Laird felt that securing the contract was a major endorsement of the skills and expertise of the shipyard and that it would safeguard and generate jobs for local people and work for local business. Construction of the flight decks took place in the giant shipbuildinghall, which is the largest in Europe, and in May 2012 they were lifted onto barges and transported to Rosyth in Scotland, where the two aircraft carriers will be assembled. The vessels are the biggest and most powerful warships ever built for the Royal Navy.

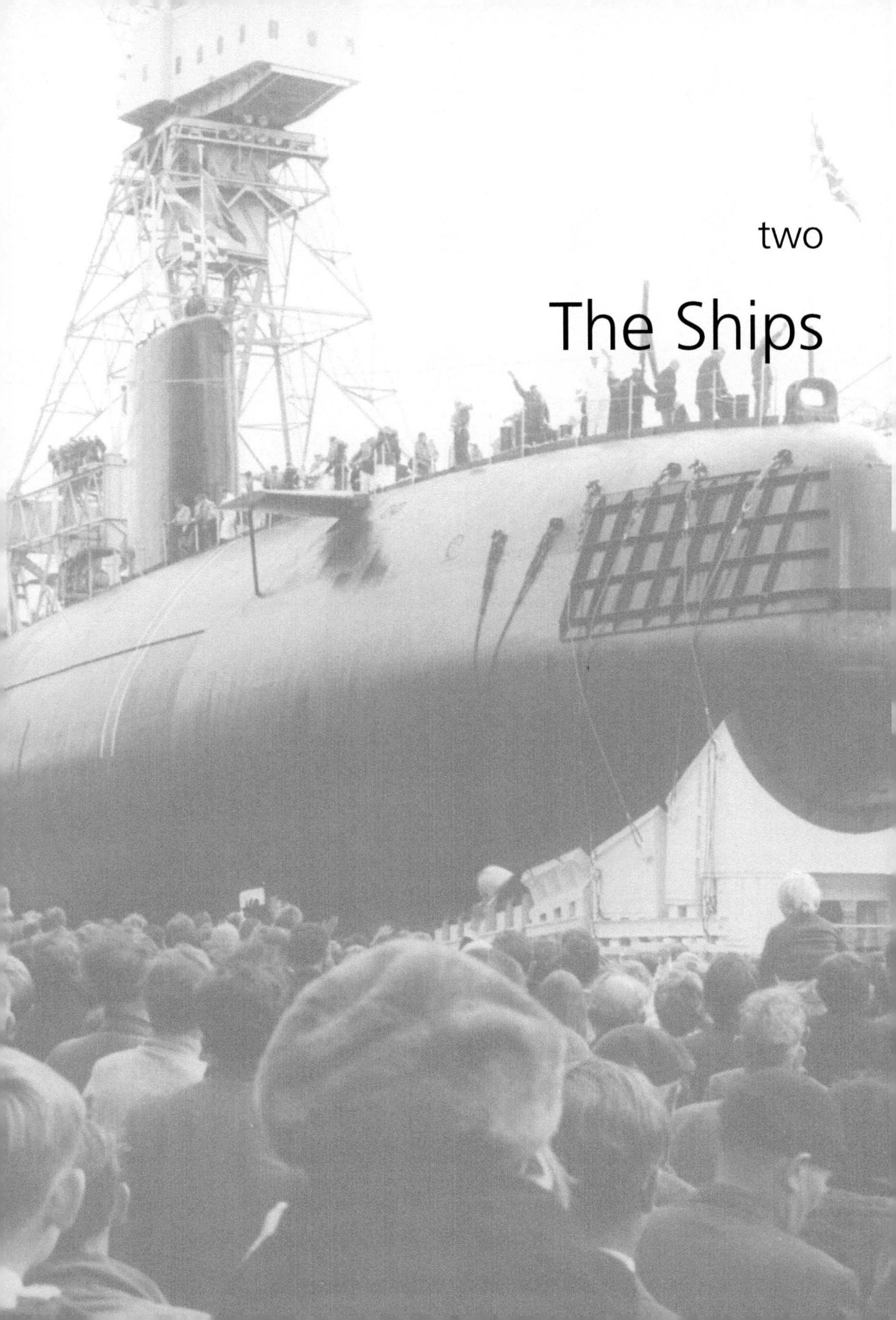

two

The Ships

Above: *HMS* Ark Royal.

Left: *HMS* Birkenhead. *(Courtesy of Wirral Archives Service)*

HMS Birkenhead 	1845 	**Royal Navy** 	**1,400 tons**
  	64m x 12m 	**12 knots** 	**No.0051**

The paddle steamer HMS *Birkenhead* was launched at Birkenhead on New Year's Day, 1845. The local newspaper described the launch, which:

> ... took place exactly at twenty minutes past eleven, and the ceremony of christening was performed by the Marchioness of Westminster. There were present, the Marquess of Westminster, the Earl of Wilton, Sir Philip and Lady Egerton, Mr Ireland Blackburn, MP and a host of the principal gentry in South Cheshire.

She was an iron-hulled ship which was driven by steam-driven paddle wheels with eight lifeboats placed next to the paddle boxes. Her armament consisted of two 96-pound first guns, one forward and the other aft, and four 68-pounder broadside guns.

On 7 January 1852, she sailed from Cork to South Africa, taking on coal at Simon's Town on 25 February, bound for Cape Town. She had 638 people, including 476 British soldiers and 20 women and children on board. On the morning of 26 February she ran aground on a rock near Danger Point between Cape Hangklip and Cape Agulhas.

A long gash in the hull caused water to rush into the ship and over one hundred soldiers drowned in their bunks. The other troops rushed up onto the decks to assist the crew to launch the lifeboats, and attempted to pump the water out of the vessel. It was only possible to free three of the boats as the others had been painted and the paint had caused them to be inoperative. Women and children were placed in the boats that could be launched when it became clear that the ship was sinking.

Lt-Col. Alexander Seton ordered his men to stay on the deck and the horses were put in the water so they could swim to the shore. The soldiers maintained their position on the deck and, when the ship sank, only 193 people survived. As the ship sank in shark-infested waters, many of the 445 people who died were attacked as they attempted to swim ashore to safety. The captain of the ship and Lt-Col. Seton were among those who perished that day.

The name of the rock that the ship collided with has been named Birkenhead Rock. The term 'women and children first' has been credited as having its roots in this tragic accident, as a tribute to the brave men and officers who died on the *Birkenhead* that day. Residents of Gansbaai, South Africa, formed the Birkenhead Commemoration Committee, which organises events to mark the anniversary.

On 26 February 2002, the Committee marked the 150th anniversary of the loss of HMS *Birkenhead* and members performed a mass wreath-laying ceremony, when local schoolchildren made 473 wreaths for the occasion. A photographic display was held at the Royal Hospital, Chelsea, and was followed by a service of remembrance. Buckingham Palace wrote to the Committee to pass on Her Majesty The Queen's gratitude for all their efforts to maintain the memorial at Danger Point.

| **Ma Robert** | **1858** | **Royal Navy** | **No.0225** |
| | **23m x 3m** | | |

Ma Robert was the Makalolo name for Mrs David Livingstone after the birth of their first son. David Livingstone had been appointed consul for East Africa at Quelimane in Mozambique and the British Government ordered a paddle steamer to be built for his use on the Zambesi River.

The ship was built in sections by MacGregor Laird at Birkenhead, and assembled at the entrance to the Zambesi River in 1858. She was able to sail up the river as far as Tete, but proved to be inadequate for the role for which she was designed. Her draft was too deep for the river, and her hull rusted and had to be caulked.

However, in 1858 he and his party did take her 200 miles up the river Shire and trekked overland to its source, becoming the first Europeans to view Lake Nyasa. The following year he took her up the Kongoni River, where she went aground on 21 December and sank. She was replaced by two new vessels, *Pioneer* and *Lady Nyasa*, and when Livingstone attempted to salvage the *Ma Robert*, he discovered that she had been set on fire early in 1863.

| **CSS Alabama** | **1862** | **Confederate Navy** | **1,050 tons** |
| | **67m x 10m** | **13 knots** | **No.0290** |

James Dunwoody Bullock, who was the Confederate naval agent in Europe, ordered *Alabama*, and she was named *Enrica* on 29 July 1862. The United States consul in London said that her construction and sale violated Britain's neutrality but, as she was a merchant vessel, she was able to leave her builders at Birkenhead. However, *Enrica* sailed to the Azores where she was armed from two supply ships, *Agrippina* and *Bahama*, and she then became the CSS *Alabama* on 24 August 1862.

On the voyage from the Azores to Newfoundland and then to the Caribbean in 1862, *Alabama* sank twenty-seven ships. She sank the schooner USS *Hatteras* south of Galveston on 11 January 1863, and in June that year she captured the *Conrad* and was commissioned as the CSS *Tuscaloosa*. She sailed to South Africa and then to Singapore in 1863, and seized nearly forty merchant vessels, returning to Cherbourg on 11 June 1864.

The Union sloop, USS *Kearsarge*, arrived at Cherbourg on 14 June, but the captain was told he was violating French neutrality and was forced to leave the port. *Alabama* sailed on 19 June and opened fire on the *Kearsarge*, but was reduced to a sinking wreck within an hour. The British vessel *Deerhound* rescued her crew.

It has been claimed that the damage caused to United States shipping by *Alabama* and her sisters was one of the reasons for the decline in their international shipping industry at the end of the nineteenth century. Hundreds of ships were transferred to foreign registry and Britain was held liable for the damage caused by the British-built ships. The claims were finally settled under the Treaty of Washington in 1871, which found that Britain had not exercised due diligence and gave an award of $15.5 million to the United States.

Above: Ma Robert.

Right: *CSS* Alabama.

*(Courtesy of Wirral
Archives Service)*

Huascar. *(Courtesy of Wirral Archives Service)*

| **Huascar** | **1865** | **Peruvian Navy** | **1,870grt** |
| | **38m x 10m** | **12 knots** | **No.0321** |

Huascar was an ironclad turret ship ordered for the Peruvian Navy during the war with Spain. She was designed by Capt. Cowper Coles with the main armament in a 22ft-diameter turret aft of the foremast. She joined the Peruvian to Chilean Sqn and was sent to Callao by R.Adm. Manuel Blanco to participate in the final hostilities with Spain but when she arrived the revolution was over.

She was captured by the supporters of Nicolas de Pierola in 1877 and, under the command of Manuel M. Carrasco, sailed to Bolivia and was involved in a battle with HMS *Shah* and HMS *Amethyst* near Ilo in Peru on 29 May that year. Together with the *Independencia*, she was involved in the blockade of Iquique by the gunboat *Covadonga* when she sank the *Esmeralda*.

Huascar was also involved in action with the Chilean vessels *Cochrane* and *Blanco* on 8 October, off Agamos Point near Antofagasta. She received around 70 direct hits which affected her steering, damaged her turret and killed 64 of her 193 crew. She was taken over by the Chilean Navy and placed on blockade duties.

She was decommissioned in 1901 and took over the role of a submarine tender from 1917 to 1930, before becoming a museum ship at Talcahuana in 1952.

HMAS Melbourne. *(Courtesy of Wirral Archives Service)*

HMAS Melbourne   1913   **Royal Australian Navy 5,400 tons**

139m x15m   **23 knots**   **No.0772**

She was launched at the yard on 30 May 1912 by Mrs Bland, daughter of Mr Barr Smith of Adelaide, and was commissioned on 18 January 1913 when she sailed on her delivery voyage to Fremantle. HMAS *Melbourne* was part of the Australian Sqn operating in the Pacific in 1914, as a counter to German fleet under Adm. von Spee, and took part in the seizure of German possessions. She covered 11,170 miles on Pacific patrols and returned to Sydney in September that year.

HMAS *Melbourne* sailed with HMAS *Sydney* and HMS *Minotaur* on 1 November from Albany, Western Australia, on convoy duties with thirty-eight merchant vessels. She left the convoy in the Indian Ocean and reached Colombo on 14 November, then sailed for Gibraltar the following day. In December she was ordered to sail for the Azores to participate in the search for the cruiser *Karlsruhe*. She sailed for Bermuda from Madeira for attachment to the North America and West Indies stations and was involved in operations to search the coastal areas of Venezuela, Colombia and Panama for the *Karlsruhe* and her attendant ship.

From January 1915 to August 1916 she was involved in patrols in the West Indies and Jamaica, operating north to Halifax and south to the Para River, Brazil. She left that station at the end of August 1916 and sailed for Devonport, arriving there on 7 September. One month later, she left for Scapa Flow as part of the Cruiser Sqn and a member of the Grand Fleet. In January 1917 she returned to Birkenhead following serious engine problems.

HMAS *Melbourne* sailed from Birkenhead on 27 June 1917 to become part of the 2nd Light Cruiser Sqn, and carried out routine patrols and exercises in the area. She sailed from Devonport in March 1919, arriving at Sydney early in May via Suez, Singapore and Darwin.

She paid off at Sydney on 5 August but was recommissioned on 14 April the following year and from 1920 to 1924 was spent in Australian coastal waters and Pacific Island duties.

On 29 September 1924 she was paid off again at Sydney until she was decommissioned on 8 October 1925, and sailed from Sydney on 23 November for Portsmouth, returning to Australia the following August.

The following three years was spent at Phillip, Westernport and Sydney, sailing from Sydney to Portsmouth on 9 February 1928. She was paid off and sold to shipbreakers at Rosyth in Scotland and was broken up in 1929.

HMS Audacious   1913   **Royal Navy**   **23,000 tons**
                           182m x 27m   **22 knots**   **No.0775**

HMS *Audacious* was laid down at Birkenhead in 1911 as a King George V Class battleship, and was launched on 14 September the following year. She was powered by four Parsons Turbines with eighteen Yarrow Boilers that gave her a speed of nearly 22 knots. She was completed in October 1913 and had a very short life of just twelve months.

On 27 October 1914 she was off Malin Head in Northern Ireland when she struck a mine that had been laid by the German vessel *Berlin*. She was on a training exercise at the time and quickly began to take in water. A line was secured from the liner *Olympic* but, as the damage was extensive, HMS *Audacious* sank.

Olympic was the sister of the *Titanic* and, together with HMS *Liverpool* and other vessels, took off the crew, apart from 250 sailors who were involved in the towing operation. When the heavy sea and wind conditions caused the line to part, HMS *Liverpool* and the cargo vessel *Thornhill* attempted to save the ship, but they were unsuccessful and the rest of the crew were taken off the vessel.

She was the first major warship to be lost in the First World War, and problems had occurred with a number of other Royal Naval vessels. Adm. Jellicoe decided that the loss of HMS *Audacious* should be covered up and the government agreed that the vessel should be left on the fleet list until after the war. However, passengers and crew on the *Olympic* had witnessed the sinking and soon stories of her sinking had appeared in the American press.

The ship is in 216ft of water, fifteen miles off Malin Head and, because of the secrecy of her sinking, the wreck was not discovered until 1995. She is upside down with holes blown in the hull from a magazine explosion and the mine.

HMS Caroline   1914   **Royal Navy**   **3,750 tons**
                                           29 knots   **No.806**

Caroline was launched on 28 January 1914 and commissioned on 4 December that year, and joined the Grand Fleet at Scapa Flow. Her oil-fired boilers drove geared steam turbines, developing 40,000 shaft hp, with four propeller shafts giving her a speed of 29 knots.

She was armed with 2x6in-, 7x4in- and 1x3in guns with two twin 21in-torpedo tubes. Her ship's company consisted of 17 officers and 272 ratings, and she spent most of the First World War as part of the 4th Light Cruiser Sqn.

Caroline was converted to her present role in 1924 as a Depot and Training Ship and is the Headquarters of Ulster Division Royal Naval Volunteer Reserve (RNVR), berthed in Alexandra Dock, Belfast.

HMS Audacious. (*Courtesy of Wirral Archives Service*)

HMS Caroline. (*Courtesy of Trevor Kidd*)

Oropesa. *(Courtesy of Wirral Archives Service)*

Library on Samaria. *(Courtesy of Wirral Archives Service)*

Oropesa	1920	**Pacific Steam**	**14,118grt**
	162m x 20m	**Navigation Co.**	**No.08351**
		14½ knots	

Oropesa was launched at the yard on 9 December 1919, and sailed on her maiden voyage from Liverpool to Rio de Janeiro and Buenos Aires on 4 September the following year. She was designed to carry 141 first-, 131 second- and 360 third-class passengers.

In 1921 she was chartered by the Royal Mail Line for the Hamburg and Southampton service to New York, but returned back to the Pacific Steam Navigation Co.'s Liverpool service late in 1922. She was converted to oil fuel in 1924 and, in 1931, she carried the Prince of Wales and Prince George to South America.

However, on her return she was laid up at Dartmouth, where she remained until she returned to service in 1937. At the outbreak of the Second World War she became a troop transport and, on 16 January 1941, she was torpedoed by the German submarine U-96 off Ireland, and sank with a loss of 113 lives.

| **Samaria** | 1921 | **Cunard Line** | **19,602grt** |
| | **190m x 22m** | **16 knots** | **No.0836** |

At the time of her launch on 27 November 1920 *Samaria* was the largest ship built at Cammell Laird, and her launch had been delayed for over six months because of industrial disputes at the yard. She sailed on her maiden voyage from Liverpool to Boston on 19 April 1922, with 347 first-class, 350 second-class and 1,600 third-class passengers. In June she had to return to Liverpool for engine repairs, returning to her service in November that year.

In 1923 she sailed on a round-the-world cruise from New York as a one-class vessel and, on her world cruise in 1924, she was the first Cunarder to pass through the Panama Canal. She took her first voyage from Liverpool to New York in 1926 and, in July 1928, she became the largest ship to visit Galway in Ireland, when passengers were taken on board for Lourdes and Fatima.

In 1939 she was converted to a troop-ship and was painted grey, retaining her Cunard-Line funnel colours. *Samaria* carried over 20,000 servicemen and steamed 250,000 miles as a troop carrier. In 1948 she carried Canadian troops from Cuxhaven to Quebec and, in 1950, she was sent to John Brown's yard on the Clyde, for her overhaul. *Samaria* sailed from Liverpool to Quebec in June 1951 and returned to Southampton to join her sister, *Scythia*, on the Southampton Le Havre to Quebec service.

In 1952 she went aground at Quebec and, in 1953, she represented the Cunard Line at the Coronation Naval Review at Spithead. On 3 December 1955 she arrived at Southampton and was laid up. She was sold to T.W. Ward the following year, and was broken up at Inverkeithing in Scotland.

Moldavia. *(Courtesy of Wirral Archives Service)*

| **Moldavia** | 1922 | **P&O Line** | **16,277grt** |
| | **174m x 22m** | **16 knots** | **No.0839** |

She was launched at Birkenhead on 1 October 1921, and sailed on her maiden voyage from London to Bombay on 13 October the following year. In 1923, she made her first voyage to Australia, and a refit in 1925 increased her tonnage to 16,436grt. At another refit in 1928, she had a second funnel fitted and her tonnage was increased again. *Moldavia* was broken up in 1938.

| **HMS Cairo** | 1919 | **Royal Navy** | **5,250 tons** |
| | **138m x 13m** | **29 knots** | **No.870** |

HMS *Cairo* was launched at Birkenhead on 19 November 1918, and commissioned by the Royal Navy in September 1919. She was converted to an anti-aircraft cruiser at Chatham Dockyard between 1938 and May 1939. She was armed with eight 4in guns, four 2-pounders and eight 5in guns and, was powered by steam turbines that drove two propellers.

In August 1942 she was part of a large convoy that sailed through the Straits of Gibraltar with the aircraft carriers HMS *Eagle* and HMS *Furious*. On 11 August HMS *Eagle* was torpedoed by a U boat and sank. The convoy was attacked again the following day and, on 13 August they reached the range of Malta's short-range fighters. *Port Chalmers*, *Rochester Castle* and *Melbourne Star* arrived safely at Malta, and *Brisbane Star* docked astern as she had been hit by a torpedo and had a large hole in her bows.

The American tanker *Ohio* had been severely damaged and two destroyers were needed to assist her into the harbour. The cruiser HMS *Nigeria*, HMS *Kenya*, the carrier HMS *Indomitable* and the cruiser HMS *Rodney* were all damaged, and HMS *Cairo* was torpedoed and sank by a single torpedo fired by the Italian submarine *Axum* on 12 August off Bizerta.

HMS Cairo. *(Courtesy of Ian and Marilin Dounphrey – Yesterday-Wirral Books)*

Submarine R11. *(Courtesy of Wirral Archives Service)*

Submarines R11	1918	**Royal Navy**	**503 tons**
and R12	**50m x 5m**	**10 knots (on surface)**	**Nos 0876 and**
		15 knots (submerged)	**0877**

They were commissioned as anti–submarine vessels and were designed to give a greater submerged than surface speed. Each submarine was built with one small diesel engine and two large electric motors, which were arranged behind each other to drive a single propeller and were fitted with 'J' Class batteries. It was found that they were very difficult to steer on the surface and the small engine proved inadequate to charge the batteries and the submarine had to return to port for these to be charged.

Fullagar. *(Courtesy of Wirral Archives Service)*

| **Fullagar** | **1920** | **Anchor Brocklebank Line** |
| | **398grt** | **No.0882** |

Fullagar was the first all-welded vessel built and was powered by an oil engine, invented and developed by Fullagar. However, the engine proved unsuccessful and it was replaced by a Beardmore diesel in 1922.

She was employed in the coastal trade around the British Isles as *Caria* and in 1925 she was sold to a Canadian cement company at British Columbia, and became *Shean*. Sold again in 1935 to a Mexican operator, she was renamed *Cedros* and remained there until August 1937 when she sank south of Ensenada.

| **De Grasse** | **1924** | **French Line** | **17,707grt** |
| | **175m x 22m** | **16 knots** | **No.0886** |

De Grasse was laid down at the yard as the *Suffren* in 1920, and was launched on 23 February 1924. She was actually completed at St Nazaire because of a strike of workers at Birkenhead, and sailed on her maiden voyage from Le Havre to New York on 21 August 1924. However, the 463 passengers were forced to return to Le Havre two days later when the shaft on one of the electric fans broke in the after boiler room. That fan was repaired, then the following day the fan on the forward boiler room also broke. *De Grasse* arrived back at Le Havre on 24 August and when the fan was repaired, she sailed again three days later.

On 10 November 1929 she hit the Pequonnock in New York, but was not damaged. Her tonnage was re-classed as 18,435grt in 1932, when some of her passenger accommodation was removed, and following the introduction of *Normandie* in 1935, she was laid up. In 1938 it was announced that she would be reconditioned to carry out a series of West Indies cruises. A swimming pool, double-deck dining room and a new sun deck were installed for the cruises to Havana, Nassau, Miami, Haiti and Jamaica.

The following year she arrived at New York, equipped with a gun turret fitted to her foredeck and 75mm guns mounted. She had sailed from Le Havre on 7 October 1939 with 281 passengers in complete secrecy. She was painted grey and in 1940 she was laid up at Bordeaux, where she was captured by the Germans and used as an accommodation ship. She spent the rest of the war at this berth and was sunk by a depth charge on 30 August 1944 as the German troops withdrew from Bordaeux.

She was refloated exactly one year later and towed to St Nazaire where she was refitted, and returned to service on 12 July 1947. When she arrived at New York on 25 July, she was the first French Line vessel to berth since the outbreak of the war and was welcomed by whistles and fireboats. There was a bittersweet atmosphere that day because when *De Grasse* arrived, the *Normandie* was in her final stages of being scrapped at a nearby pier.

In 1952 *De Grasse* sailed from Le Havre to West Indies and was sold the following year to become the *Empress of Australia* for Canadian Pacific Steamships. The line required a passenger vessel to replace the *Empress of Canada* that had been lost following a dockside fire at Liverpool's Gladstone Dock. She sailed on her maiden voyage for them from Liverpool–Quebec on 28 April 1953, and served the line until 1956 when she was sold to Sicula Oceanica, Palermo, and renamed *Venezuela*.

She was placed on their Naples–La Guaira migrant service and in 1960 was refitted with a new bow that increased her length to 187m, and she was certified to carry 180 first-class, 500 tourist- and 800 third-class passengers. On 17 March 1962 she got stranded on rocks near Cannes and her passengers and crew were taken off the ship. The following month she was refloated and, following an inspection, it was decided that it was uneconomical to repair her and she was sold to shipbreakers at Le Spezia.

De Grasse. *(Courtesy of Wirral Archives Service)*

HMS Rodney. *(Courtesy of Wirral Archives Service)*

HMS Rodney　　　　**1927**　　　　**Royal Navy**　　　　**33,950 tons**
　　　　　　　　　　　217m x 32m　　　**23 knots**　　　　**No.0904**

HMS *Rodney* was laid down at the yard in December 1922 and was launched on 17 December 1925. She entered service with the Royal Navy in 1927. She and her sister, HMS *Nelson*, were the last battleships designed by Sir E.Tennyson D'Eyncourt, and were the reduced editions of the 48,000 ton battle cruisers ordered in 1921. The grouping of the main armament forward allowed for a minimum length of armoured citadel with maximum protection to hull and magazines. The design was governed by constructional rather than tactical principles, and the placing of the boiler room abaft of the engine rooms meant that smoke interference with the control positions was obviated.

The bridge carried 16in-, 6in- and 4.7in-directors, admiral's bridge, torpedo controls and signalling and navigating bridge. The high freeboard of the two ships was useful in heavy weather and did not affect their efficiency. The steering gear was innovative as the rudder could be swung over in 30 seconds and some of the material used in both ships was originally ordered for the two battle cruisers whose construction was abandoned in 1919.

She was refitted in 1941 and was in action with *King George V* in May 1941 when they sank *Bismarck*. On 24 May HMS *Hood* opened fire on *Bismarck* in the Denmark Strait and *Bismarck* was hit on the port side by three shells from *Prince of Wales*. In the action, *Hood* blew up and sank, and *Bismarck* took three direct hits from *Prince of Wales*. *Bismarck* reported that *Hood* sunk and that she had no electrics, the port boiler room was taking water, and that she intended to head for St Nazaire.

The following day, *Bismarck* was attacked by HMS *Victorious* and the next day she was sighted by HMS *Sheffield* and attacked by fourteen Swordfish aircraft and hit by two torpedoes. She reported that she was rudderless and no longer manoeuvrable. The next day in force 8-9 conditions, she was sighted by battleships *King George V* and *Rodney*, who opened fire. After a fierce battle, most of *Bismarck*'s turrets were hit and disabled and a torpedo fired from *Dorsetshire* also hit her. At 10.39 a.m. she sank and the British vessels rescued 116 men from the water. HMS *Rodney* was placed in reserve in 1945 and decommissioned the following year. She was finally sold for scrap and arrived at Inverkeithing on 26 March 1948.

Almeda. *(Courtesy of Wirral Archives Service)*

Almeda	**1926**	**Blue Star Line**	**12,838grt**
	163m x 21m	**17 knots**	**No.0919**

Almeda was launched on 29 June 1926 and was the first of three similar sister ships built for the Blue Star Line's London–South America passenger services. She had accommodation for 180 first-class passengers and was also designed to carry general and refrigerated cargo. She sailed on her maiden voyage from London on 16 February 1927 and in 1929 was renamed *Almeda Star*.

In 1935 she was lengthened by 20m and her capacity was reduced to 150 first-class passengers. On 28 May 1937 she went aground at Boulogne and was refloated. Later that year her mainmast was removed. She was badly damaged during an air raid in Liverpool on 22 December 1940, and required extensive damage repairs. On 17 January 1941 she was sailing west of the Outer Hebrides and was attacked by the German submarine U-86, and sank. As the attack occurred during a severe gale, all 194 passengers and 166 crew were lost.

Andalucia was launched at the yard on 21 September 1926 for Blue Star Line's service from London–South America. In 1929 she became the *Andulucia Star* and was lengthened in 1937, with her passenger accommodation being reduced from 180 to 150 first-class berths. On 7 October 1942 she was torpedoed and sank by the German submarine U-107, approximately 400 miles west of Monrovia.

The *Arandora* entered service on the London–South America service in May 1927. The following year she was converted to a cruise liner on the Clyde, and was renamed *Arandora Star*. In 1931 her hull was painted white and during the 1930s she received two extensive refits and her superstructure was extended to her poop deck.

In 1939 she was taken over by the Admiralty and became a troop-ship. On 2 July 1940 she left Liverpool on a voyage to Canada, with 1,178 German and Italian prisoners of war on board and 430 crew. The following day, a torpedo from the submarine U-47 hit her when she was seventy-five miles west of Ireland. *Arandora Star* sank within an hour of being attacked, with 761 people losing their lives. The survivors were picked up by the Canadian destroyer, *St Laurent*.

<table>
<tr><td>Ben-My-Chree</td><td>1927
111m x 14m</td><td>Isle of Man Steam
Packet Co.
22 knots</td><td>2586grt.
No.0926</td></tr>
</table>

Ben-My-Chree was launched on 5 April 1927 and sailed on her trials on 21 June, achieving a speed of 22.8 knots. Her maiden voyage from Liverpool–Douglas took place on 29 June, when she took 2 hours 27 minutes from the Bar Lightship to Douglas with an average speed of 22.4 knots. She collided with *Snaefell* in August that year, and both vessels were sent to the Mersey for repairs.

In 1932 she was chartered by the Diocese of Blackburn to take passengers to the Eucharistic Conference in Dublin, and her hull was painted white. The charter was later cancelled as her sleeping accommodation was thought to be insufficient, but she retained her white hull. The *Lady of Mann* was painted white in 1933 and the *Mona's Queen* was launched with a white hull and green boot topping.

Between 1941 and 1944, the *Ben-My-Chree* was used as a troop transport between Britain and Iceland. She was converted at North Shields in 1944 to carry six landing craft and was Headquarters ship for the 514th Assault Flotilla at Omaha Beach. At the end of the Second World War she returned to Birkenhead, berthing at Morpeth Dock on 11 May 1946. Work was completed on her by Cammell Laird which enabled her to return to service on 6 July, and she was returned to them at the end of the season for an extensive overhaul.

Her cowl was removed from her funnel during her overhaul in 1950, which altered her appearance, and in the winter of 1957/58, Cammell Laird completed a major refit on the vessel. The '*Ben*' remained in service until 13 September 1965, when she sailed from Douglas–Liverpool on her final passenger voyage for the Steam Packet.

On her return to the Mersey she was laid up in Morpeth Dock. The suffix '11' was added to allow the new car ferry being constructed by Cammell Laird to be given the name. She was sold to Van Heyghen Freres and was towed to Antwerp by the tug *Fairplay XI* and arrived at Bruges on 23 December 1965 to be broken up.

Ben-My-Chree.

Greystoke Castle.
(Courtesy of Wirral Archives Service)

Greystoke Castle	1927	**James Chambers**	**5,853grt**
	134m x 17m	13 knots	No. 0928

Greystoke Castle was delivered to the Lancashire Shipping Co. in 1927 and was purchased by the Elder Dempster Line in 1943, and became *Freetown* at the end of the Second World War. On 31 January 1948 she grounded at Northfleet but was soon afloat again. However, she then collided with the Cory vessel *Corcrest*, killing two of the crew, and then also collided with the *Yewcroft*. She was sold for scrapping at Hamburg in 1958.

Her sister, *Penrith Castle*, was launched on 9 May 1929 for James Chambers, and delivered to the Lancashire Shipping Co. In 1943 she was bought by the Elder Dempster Line and retained the same name. In 1946 she was renamed *Fantee* and, on 10 October 1949 on a voyage from Amsterdam–Liverpool, she grounded off the Scilly Isles and broke in two. All the crew were rescued and saved.

The third sister, *Thurland Castle*, was launched at the yard on 26 March 1929, and was also sold to the Elder Dempster Line in 1943. She was renamed *Fulani* in 1946 and was damaged by fire in Brunswick Dock, Liverpool, while loading cargo for West Africa on 21 June 1950. In 1958 she was sold for breaking up at Odense.

BOOTH LINE

to

BARBADOS
TRINIDAD

via
LEIXOES (Oporto) LISBON
MADEIRA
and return

R.M.S. "Hubert" : First Class Smoking Room

R.M.S. "Hubert" : First Class Double Cabin with Private Bathroom and Toilet

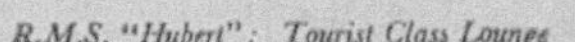

R.M.S. "Hubert" : Tourist Class Lounge

FIRST AND TOURIST CLASS ACCOMMODATION

EXCELLENT CUISINE

SPORTS DECK

Booth Line sailing line brochure for their services from Liverpool to South America.

Hilary.

Hilary   **1931**   **Booth Steam**   **7,403grt**
             129m x 17m   **Ship Co.**   **14 knots**
                                             No.0975

Hilary was launched on 17 April 1931, and sailed on her maiden voyage from Liverpool to Para and Manaus. She served the company on their South American routes until 1940, when she became an Ocean Boarding Vessel as HMS *Hilary*, and was converted for that role at South Shields on the Tyne.

She saw service in the North Atlantic and, on 3 May 1941, she intercepted the Italian tanker *Recco* near the Azores. The crew scuttled the ship and the tanker sank. Several days later she captured another Italian vessel, the *Gianna M*, and she was taken into Belfast. In 1942 she became the convoy commodore ship, and in October that year, a torpedo which failed to detonate struck her.

In 1943 she was used as an infantry landing ship and had six assault craft fitted to her boat deck by Cammell Laird. In July that year, she was the invasion Headquarters of Rear Admiral Sir Philip Vian for Operation 'Husky', the invasion of Sicily. In September she was the Headquarters of the invasion of Salerno under Commodore G.N. Oliver, and in 1944 she was the Headquarters of the invasion of Normandy.

She was refitted by Cammell Laird in 1945 and returned to service with accommodation for 93 first- and 138 tourist-class passengers. In 1956 she received an overhaul at Antwerp and was painted with a white hull. On her return to the Mersey she was placed on Elder Dempster's West African service to Lagos, but returned to the Booth Line service in 1957. On 12 September 1959 she sailed from Liverpool on her final sailing and was sold to Thos.W. Ward to be broken up at Inverkeithing.

St Andrew	1932	**Fishguard &**	**2,702 grt**
	100m x 14m	**Rosslare Railway**	**No.0981**
	22 knots	**& Harbour Co.**	

St Andrew was built in 1932 for service on the Fishguard–Rosslare route, which she maintained until the outbreak of the Second World War. She was converted to a hospital ship in 1939 with accommodation for 267 patients, 58 medical staff and 93 crew. Her base was Newhaven which was classed as BEF No.1 Ambulance Port, and she was joined there by ten ex-railway hospital ships.

On 30 May 1940 she took part in the evacuation of Dunkirk, assisting in bringing troops back to Britain from France. She was transferred to duties in the Mediterranean in 1943, and was based at Malta and attacked by the enemy on fifteen occasions. On 13 September 1943 she was in the company of three other hospital ships, *Tairea*, *Leinster* and *Newfoundland*, and when they were attacked, *Newfoundland* sank. *St Andrew* searched the area and saved over 100 people, mostly American nurses.

She was damaged at Anzio during the Italian campaign in January 1944, making thirty-seven trips to and from the beach head. She also served at Bari and along the Adriatic Coast to Ancona later in the war. In September 1944 she collided with a mine and had to be towed to Taranto to be repaired. At the end of the war she returned to Birkenhead for a major overhaul and was converted back into a cross-channel ferry, and reopened the service from Fishguard–Rosslare in 1946. She remained on this service and was converted into a side loader for cars in 1965, and was replaced by the *Duke of Rothesay* in 1967, when she was sold and broken up.

St Andrew.

HMS Fearless. *(Courtesy of Wirral Archives Service)*

HMS Fearless	**1934**	**Royal Navy**	**1,375 tons**
		14 knots	**No.0992**

She was an 'F' Class destroyer which was launched at Birkenhead on 12 May 1934, and was commissioned in December that year. She was armed with four 4.7in guns and eight 21in-torpedo tubes. In 1937 she was in action during the Spanish Civil War and, in 1940 she and HMS *Brazen* sank the German submarine U–49 off Harstadt. The following year she helped sink the submarine U–38, west of Cape Trafalgar, but suffered torpedo damage a month later from an Italian aircraft, while attempting to protect HMS *Ark Royal*. *Fearless* caught fire and lost all power, and when the damage was inspected it was decided that it was too extensive, and the crew were taken off. *Forester* sank her on 23 July 1941.

Clement. *(Courtesy of Wirral Archives Service)*

| **Clement** | 1934 | **Booth Line** | 5.051grt |
| | 126m x 17m | 13 knots | No.1,000 |

Clement was the 1,000th ship to be completed by Cammell Laird at Birkenhead and entered service for Booth Line's service to South America in 1934. However, she also had a very short life as she was sunk in the early months of the Second World War.

She left New York on a voyage to Brazil on 19 August 1939 and, when she reached Pernambuco on 30 September, she was captured by the German Heavy Cruiser *Admiral Graf Spee*, and sank.

The German vessel sank eight more ships in the next two months until HMS *Exeter*, *Ajax* and *Achilles* drove her into Montevideo. The master of the *Admiral Graf Spee*, Commander Langsdorf, scuttled the vessel and the crew abandoned the ship. As the ship was sinking, Commander Langsdorf shot himself.

| **Ark Royal** | 1938 | **Royal Navy** | 28,480 tons |
| | 244m x 29m | 31 knots | No.1,012 |

Ark Royal was launched on 13 April 1937 and was completed at the yard in November the following year. She was the first British naval vessel to be designed and built as an aircraft carrier, and was powered by Parson-geared turbines with six Admiralty three-drum boilers, which gave her a speed of 31 knots. She was built to carry 60 aircraft and was armed with 16x4.5in guns, 32x2-pounders and 32x0.5in guns, and had a crew of 1,600 men.

One of her first missions was in December 1939 when she was sent to the South Atlantic to help search for the German cruiser *Graf Spee* and, early in 1940, she took part in the Norwegian campaign. In July that year she participated in the attack on the French Naval Base at Mers El Kebir in Algeria, and in September she was involved in the second assault on the French Navy at Dakar.

On 14 November 1941 the German U-81 torpedoed HMS *Ark Royal* when a single torpedo hit the vessel on the starboard side. As the hit was amidships it caused four main compartments and over 30m of the ship's starboard bilge to flood. The torpedo created a hole 40m long by 10m deep, causing the starboard boiler room, air spaces, the main switchboard, oil tanks and the lower steering position to flood. She soon started to list, increasing from 10° to 18° in 20 minutes.

The captain assessed the situation and, because of the severity of the damage, he decided to evacuate the ship and brought all the engineering staff on deck. As some covers and hatches were not secured during the evacuation, the ship took on more water and more of the boiler rooms were flooded and shut down. An hour and 19 minutes after the direct hit, all the power failed and most of the crew were ordered to abandon the ship. However, a small number of crew were placed on repair and assessment duties and attempted to keep the vessel afloat.

The engineers who remained on board fought to re-open the ship's power plant and, after five hours, the plant was again operating. As the list had increased to 18° by then, the water began to spread across the whole width of the ship in the boiler room flat and the boiler room shut down again. Eleven hours after the hit, the list was 20° and an hour later, this had increased to 27° and the captain gave the order to abandon ship. When the list reached 45°, HMS *Ark Royal* capsized and sank.

An Inquiry into the sinking conducted after the war concluded that the main cause of the loss was inexperience and poor judgement of the officers responsible for damage control, and a lack of initiative by them. The proper damage control measures were not taken and consideration was not given in time to tow the vessel to Gibraltar, which was

Ark Royal. *(Courtesy of Wirral Archives Service)*

less than twenty-five miles away. The Inquiry concluded that if proper applications of counter-flooding and standard damage control procedures had been taken, the ship would have been saved.

The Inquiry also found that the uninterrupted boiler room flat was a significant error that was immediately rectified in the Illustrious and Indefatigable classes, the adoption of a double hangar had forced the use of cross-deck uptakes low in the ship, adding to vulnerability, the reliance of steam generators was also an error and the power train design was strongly criticised.

HMS Prince of Wales   1941   **Royal Navy**   **43,786 tons**
                            227m x 34m **28½ knots**   **No.1,026**

HMS *Prince of Wales* was launched on 3 May 1939 by the Princess Royal and in 1940 a German bomb narrowly missed her when it exploded next to her at the yard. She sustained very light damage and slightly flooded some of her compartments. She was commissioned on 31 March 1941, and sailed the following month for trials and crew training.

Early in her career she was involved in the pursuit of the German battleship *Bismarck* in the Denmark Strait. She suffered mechanical difficulties during the battle and received a direct hit to the compass platform that resulted in the death of fourteen men. She returned after the battle for repairs and in August that year she carried the British Prime Minister, Winston Churchill, to Newfoundland, to meet the President of the United States, Franklin D. Roosevelt, to discus the Atlantic Charter.

On her return she was part of Operation 'Halberd' with *Rodney*, *Nelson* and the aircraft carrier *Ark Royal*, escorting a convoy from Gibraltar to Malta. Italian aircraft attacked the convoy and the *Prince of Wales* shot down two fighter aircraft. In October 1941 she was sent to Singapore via Freetown, Sierra Leone, Cape Town and Colombo. On 10 December she was sunk by a Japanese torpedo and bomber aircraft off Kuantan, Malaya, with a loss of life of 280 sailors and 27 marines, including Adm. Sir Tom Phillips, Commander in Chief of the Eastern Fleet, and HMS *Prince of Wales* Captain John C. Leach. In his memoirs, Winston Churchill said that he felt sad to think that half the crew of *Prince of Wales* who attended the meeting with President Roosevelt for the Atlantic Conference would die within a year.

Thetis   1939   **Royal Navy**   **82m x 8m**
                            9 knots   **No.1,027**

On 1 June 1939, the submarine *Thetis* sailed from the yard under the command of Lt-Com. G.H. Bolus to undertake a diving trial. On board were 103 people, nearly double her normal compliment. Some of the extra people on board were naval officers who were submarine captains, and were there to see the new vessel in action. The others were engine fitters, electricians and shipyard workers employed by Cammell Laird and Vickers Armstrong. Two employees of a catering firm and the pilot were also on board that day.

Two months earlier it had been discovered, while she was on trials, that the steering gear had been connected the wrong way round. The yard and Admiralty had planned to take her to the Clyde for a diving trial but because of the steering problems this was cancelled.

Right: Prince of Wales.

Below: Thetis.

Thetis was escorted by the Liverpool Screw Towing & Lighterage tug, *Grebe Cock*, which was to take the passengers off the submarine prior to the diving trials. At 1.30 p.m., *Thetis* signalled to the tug that the passengers had decided to remain on board and that they would proceed with the dive. The tanks were emptied of air at 2.00 p.m and she took nearly an hour to disappear below the surface. Observers on the tug said that she had her bow at an unusual angle and, at 2.58 p.m. she suddenly went down.

When the dive commenced, it was found that the submarine was light and needed more weight so more water had to be brought on board. Nos 5 and 6 forward tubes were checked, as these should have been filled with water in the absence of torpedoes. The bow cap was opened to let the water in and it was confirmed that the rear door was closed, otherwise the submarine would flood. There were inspection holes on this rear door and unfortunately these had been painted over, which created a seal in the door.

The rear inspection lever was opened and it was concluded that there was very little water in No.5 tube. The cover was opened and water gushed in and some of the men were knocked off their feet, but the forward compartment had now been flooded. The bow dropped deeper in the water and at the same time the engines were given more power, causing the vessel to sink to the bottom. The men tried to close the hatch in the forward compartment but were unsuccessful, and the two forward compartments flooded.

She had sufficient safety equipment for all persons on board and sufficient air for 36 hours but, as she had double the number on board, this was reduced to 18 hours. It was planned that *Thetis* would surface after 15 minutes and, when this did not happen, the *Grebe Cock* signalled that that they suspected that all was not well. The tug eventually drifted over four miles away from the submarine.

When the stern tubes were emptied on *Thetis*, her stern was raised and was over 18ft out of the water, and the after escape hatch was 20ft below the water. It was now dark and the crew of *Thetis* waited for signs that rescue vessels were in the area. At 7.45 a.m. an aircraft searching the area noticed the stern sticking out of the water. This was 18 hours since she had gone down and the amount of oxygen on board was at its limit.

Ships were soon at the scene and messages were hammered on the stern to let the men know that the rescue operation was commencing. The escape chamber was flooded to allow the first to men to come to the surface. Unfortunately, they were both dead; two further attempts were made and four men were brought to the surface. Hawsers were attached to the submarine but when the two escape hatches were opened at the same time, the sea flooded the vessel. This caused the hawsers to part and *Thetis* sank again to the seabed. It took several months to raise *Thetis* then she was beached and most of the men were buried in a mass grave at Holyhead on Angelsey.

Thetis was salvaged, repaired and renamed HMS *Thunderbolt*. On 14 March 1943 she was depth charged by the Italian vessel *Cicogna*, and sank in the Mediterranean.

| **Mauretania** | **1939** | **Cunard Steamship Co.** | **35,739grt** |
| | **235m x 27m** | **23 knots** | **No.1,029** |

When her keel was laid in 1937, *Mauretania* became the largest liner to be built in England and was the first passenger liner to be constructed for the Cunard–White Star Line. She was built without any Government subsidy and was designed to relieve the *Queen Mary* when required. She was launched at the yard on 28 July 1938 from slipway No.6. The following March she sailed out of the Mersey on her acceptance trials, achieving an average speed of 22 knots.

Her maiden voyage took place on 17 June 1939, when large crowds on both sides of the Mersey saw her sail from the Pier Head to New York. In August that year she was transferred to London–New York service and became the largest vessel to use the King George V dock. On 14 September she made a voyage from Southampton–New York, returning to Liverpool and, after another round trip she sailed to New York where she was laid up on 16 December 1939.

In March 1940 she became a troop-ship and sailed from New York–Sydney via the Panama Canal and Honolulu for conversion. On 5 May she sailed from Sydney to the Clyde, with over 2,000 troops. Over the period of the Second World War, *Mauretania* made forty-eight trooping voyages covering 540,000 miles, and carried over 355,000 troops.

She arrived back on the Mersey on 2 August 1946 to be converted back to a passenger liner at Gladstone Dock, Liverpool by Cammell Laird & Co. On 18 April the following year, when the work was completed, she left Liverpool on a 2½ day short cruise but, because of bad weather, she was unable to return until five days later. However, on 26 April she restarted the Liverpool–New York service, and later transferred to Southampton.

In 1957 she was fitted with air-conditioning during her overhaul so she was able to undertake a programme of cruises, including around-the-world voyages. During her winter overhaul in 1962, she was painted in 'Caronia' green, and the following year she was placed on the New York–Cannes–Genoa–Naples service. Her final sailing on this service was on 15 September 1965, and she returned to Southampton where she was sold to be broken up. She arrived at Inverkeithing on 23 November to be scrapped by Thos. W. Ward.

Mauretania.

HMS Charybdis. *(Courtesy of Wirral Archives Service)*

HMS Charybdis   **1941**   **Royal Navy**   **No.1,041**

She was a cruiser of the Dido Class that was ordered under the 1938 programme, and was laid down at the yard on 9 November 1938. HMS *Charybdis* was launched on 17 September 1940, and handed over to the Admiralty on 3 December the following year.

Following the completion of successful trials, she joined the Home Fleet and was involved in mine-laying. She sailed for Gibraltar and was transferred to the North Atlantic Command and, that year she was involved in providing cover for the Malta convoys in Operation 'Harpoon', involving aircraft reinforcements for the island.

She was transferred to patrol duties in the Atlantic, and searching for German raiders and blockade-runners at the beginning of October 1942, moving back to covering aircraft reinforcements to Malta later that month. On 25 November she was allocated to the 12th Cruiser Sqn, sailing from Gibraltar to Algiers with the Allied Forces Headquarters for Operation 'Torch', which was the invasion of French North Africa. On completion of these duties she was transferred back to the Home Fleet.

Early in 1943 she was at Scapa Flow on mine-laying duties and patrolling in the North Sea, and in April she moved to the Plymouth Command to cover convoys and patrol in the Bay of Biscay. In August 1943 she was back at Gibraltar escorting Mediterranean convoys and in September she was involved in the Salerno Landings, and returned to Plymouth the following month.

On 23 October 1943 she was taking part in Operation 'Tunnel', and was torpedoed by German destroyers *T-23* and *T-27*. She sank with the loss of life of 30 officers and 432 ratings.

HMS Thrasher   1941   Royal Navy   82m x 8m
9 knots   No.1,050

The submarine HMS *Thrasher* was laid down at the yard on the 14 November 1939, was launched on the 28 November 1940, and commissioned the following year. She was a member of the 'Triton' Class and, it was with this class that the Royal Navy decided to name submarines rather that give them numbers. *Triton* was built by Vickers Armstrong at Barrow-in-Furness, and the second of the class was *Thetis*. Fifteen members of the group one were built, six of group two and thirty-four of group three.

Group one submarines had riveted hulls, some of group two had welded hulls and all of group three were welded. The forward end of the submarine contained six internal torpedo tubes, loaded and ready for firing, and three torpedoes each side stored in their racks. Aft of this section was the crew's accommodation and messes. Through the third bulkhead was the control room, which was always the heart of a submarine. The control room housed the two periscopes, gyrocompass, ASDIC listening posts, helmsman posts and had access to the turret tower.

The fourth bulkhead contained the engine and motor room with two diesel engines and two electric motors. The fifth bulkhead was used by the stokers and contained machinery for steering the submarine, and was also used for torpedo storage. Air-conditioning units were installed, taking air through a cooling drying plant before going through the normal ventilation pipes.

The main machinery was the diesel engines for surface propulsion and electric motors when submerged. Vickers-built members of the class used a Vickers engine; Cammell Laird vessels were fitted with Swiss-made Sulzer engines; Scotts used German super-charged engines and the Royal Dockyard-built submarines had Admiralty engines. Each battery consisted of 336 cells, with each cell weighing over half a ton. Fully charged, each battery would last for forty-eight hours at 2½ knots, and at a top speed of 9 knots they would only last an hour.

Each submarine had a 4in gun mounted on the conning tower, which was sited inside a metal housing with large drainage holes in the bottom. On either side of the pressure hull were the main ballast tanks, which filled when submerging, and compressed air forced the water out of these when the submarine surfaced.

HMS Thrasher. (Courtesy of Wirral Archives Service)

In July 1941 *Thrasher* stopped 70m off the beach of Limni in southern Crete and rescued seventy military and Greek personnel from under the nose of the Germans. The servicemen were Australian, and New Zealanders, and they were taken to safety at Alexandria.

On the 13/14 January 1942 *Thrasher* was attacked and sank a supply ship off northern Crete. She was attacked again and, when she surfaced that night, two unexploded bombs were discovered in the forward casing. Lt Roberts and Petty Officer Gould removed the first bomb but, as the other was lying in a confined space, Petty Officer Gould had to lay on his back with the bomb in his arms while the Lieutenant dragged him back by his shoulders. It took them 40 minutes to get the bomb clear and drop it over the side, and they were clearly in danger of the bomb exploding. As they were on deck all the time they would have been sacrificed if the enemy had attacked the submarine. Both men received the Victoria Cross for this action.

At the end of the war the class was to be modernised, but only five were streamlined, given six-bow tubes only and a modern sonar, and fin-type conning tower. They were *Tapir*, *Tireless*, *Talent*, *Teredo* and *Token*. *Tabard*, *Truant*, *Truncheon*, *Tiptoe*, *Taciturn*, *Thermopylae*, *Totem* and *Turpin* were completely rebuilt and streamlined between 1950 and 1956 with a fin-type conning tower, and improved diesel-electric propulsion was also fitted.

| **Salveda** | **1943** | **HM Government** | **728 tons** |
| | | | **No.1,111** |

Salveda was launched on 9 February 1943 for the Admiralty as a single screw, steam-engined salvage tug, and was managed between 1943 and 1946 by the Liverpool and Glasgow Salvage Association. In 1947 she was chartered to Metal Industries at Glasgow and based in the north of Scotland on salvage duties, and was laid up in 1966 in the reserve fleet. In February 1972 she was sold by Pounds Shipowners and Shipbreakers Limited of Portsmouth to G. Vamvounakis of Greece, and was refitted by Husband's Shipyard at Southampton. She was scrapped in 1973.

Salveda. *(Courtesy of Wirral Archives Service)*

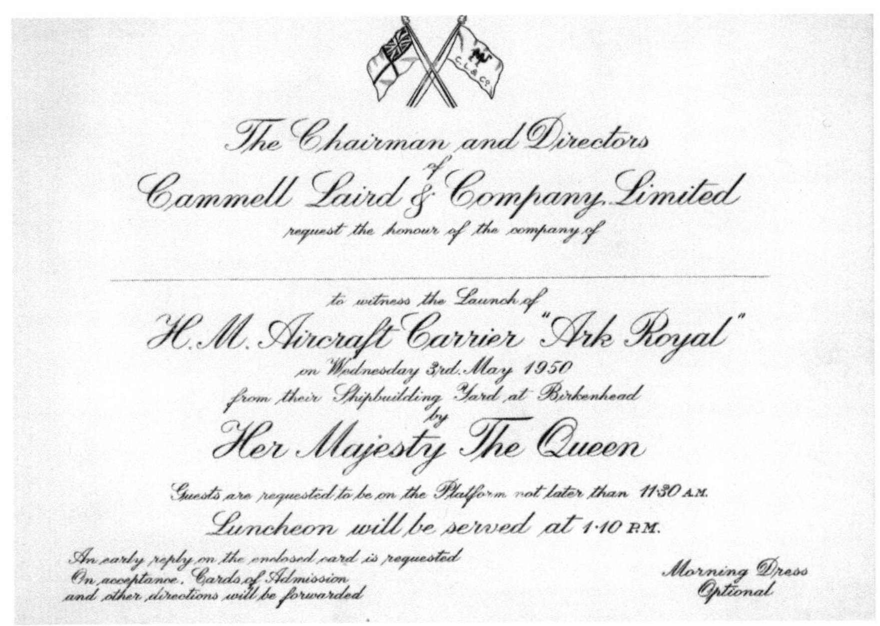

Launch ticket for HMS Ark Royal *on 3 May 1950.*

| **HMS Ark Royal** | **1955** | **Royal Navy** | **53,060 tons** |
| | **220m x 34m** | **32 knots** | **No.1,119** |

HMS *Ark Royal* was laid down as *Audacious* in 1943, but work on her was suspended at the end of the war when the plans were modernised. She became the Royal Navy's first large post-war aircraft carrier and was completed with an angled deck, enlarged island and a new system of electronics. She was launched on the 3 May 1950 by Her Majesty Queen Elizabeth, and was finally completed and handed over on 26 February 1955.

She was powered by Parsons geared turbines with eight boilers and four shafts giving a top speed of 32 knots. *Ark Royal* was refitted between 21 July 1958 and 28 December 1959, when her armaments were reduced and the number of aircraft carried was revised to forty-eight from fifty units. She received her first major refit between 1966 and 1970, when all the guns were removed and she was fitted with the ability to carry four Seacat missiles, but they were never actually installed on her. The number of aircraft carried on her was again reduced, to thirty-six units.

Ark Royal was out of service for refitting between July 1973 and April 1974, and October 1976 and May 1977, and she suffered a continual maintenance problem throughout her time in service with the navy. She was the last conventional aircraft carrier operating conventional fighter and attack aircraft, and had a stores ship assigned to her to cater for the logistical needs and the aircraft.

It was clear by the early 1970s that the maintenance problems were causing her to be unreliable, and a decision to scrap her was made by the middle of that decade. However, as her replacement was cancelled, she was not decommissioned until 4 December 1978, and was finally sold in 1980 to be broken up.

HMS Springer
HMS Sanguine

1945	Royal Navy	715 tons
66m x 7m	14 knots	Nos 1,142
		and 1,140

In the 1920s and early 1930s, the Admiralty decided to order two main types of patrol submarines. One was a medium-sized type for confined waters and the other was slightly larger that would be used for other duties. It was resolved that the submarines would have their fuel tanks internally built and would have the quick diving and manageable handling of the 'H' Class, together with the long range qualities of the 'O', 'P' and 'R' Classes.

The new submarine was the 'S' Class and became the largest group of submarines ever built for the Royal Navy. *Salmon, Sealion* and *Spearfish* were built at Birkenhead between 1933 and 1937, and the yard delivered thirty-two 'S' Class vessels between 1940 and 1945. *Springer* was launched on 14 May 1945, *Sanguine* on 15 February that year, and both were commissioned in 1945.

In 1958 HMS *Springer* and HMS *Sanguine* were sold to the government of Israel, and the first Prime Minister of Israel, David Ben-Gurion, gave them new Hebrew names. *Springer* became *Tanin* and *Sanguine* was renamed *Rahav*. They were refitted at Birkenhead in August 1959 and, following trials they sailed for Portsmouth, and then to Haifa. On 16 December *Tanin* arrived at Haifa, followed by *Rahav* several months later.

Tanin took part in the Six-Day War in June 1967, and carried naval commandoes to attack the port of Alexandria. She also attacked an Egyptian ship and was damaged in the depth charge attack that followed. They returned to port when the war finished, and were decommissioned. *Rahav* was sold to the shipbreakers in 1969 and, in 1972, *Tanin* was used as a target for a torpedo from the Israeli Naval Ship *Dolphin*.

HMS Springer.

Ellerman Hall and City Lines Sailing list for City of Bristol.

Sacramento	**1945**	**Ellerman's**	**7,096 grt**
	137m x 18m	**Wilson Line**	**No.1,160**
		14 knots	

She was built as *Sacramento* for Ellerman's Wilson Line and was transferred to the Ellerman & Bucknall Line in 1964, when she was renamed *City of Bristol*. In 1969 she was sold to Anna Shipping Co. of Famagusta, when her funnel height was raised and she became *Felicie*. In 1970 she was sold to the Republic of Cuba, renamed *30 de Novembre* and operated by Lineas Mambisa (Empresa Consolidada de Nav. Mambisa, Havana). She remained in service until 1977, when she was sold to shipbreakers at Faslane in Scotland.

City of Bristol, *formerly* Sacramento.

BLUE STAR LINE

LISBON & SOUTH AMERICA

CARRYING H.M. MAILS

S.S. "PARAGUAY STAR"

FOR

LISBON	TENERIFFE
Due 24th Dec.	Due 27th Dec.
RIO DE JANEIRO	SANTOS
Due 5th Jan.	Due 7th Jan.
MONTEVIDEO	BUENOS AIRES
Due 10th Jan.	Due 11th Jan.

Receiving Cargo at

No. 16 SHED, ROYAL ALBERT DOCK, LONDON

From 13th Dec. until 18th Dec.

REFRIGERATED SPACE AVAILABLE

CARGO FOR BRAZIL AND URUGUAY MUST BE SPECIALLY BOOKED BEFORE DELIVERY

All Bills of Lading MUST be lodged by closing date

NEXT SAILING

m.v. "IBERIA STAR" closing for cargo 1st Jan.

INSURANCE EFFECTED AT COMPETITIVE RATES

For further particulars, rates of freight, etc. apply:—

BLUE STAR LINE

LTD.

ALBION HOUSE, LEADENHALL STREET, LONDON, E.C.3

TELEPHONE: ROYAL 4567

BIRMINGHAM 6 Victoria Square   MANCHESTER 556 Royal Exchange

GLASGOW 93 Hope Street

Passenger Office: 3 LOWER REGENT STREET LONDON, S.W.1   (For other Agents see overleaf)

Left: *Blue Star Line Sailing List.*

Below: Fiesta.

Opposite below: *SS* Argentina Star *games deck.*

Fiesta

Fiesta was built in 1946 as *Mona's Queen* (yard No.1173) for the Isle of Man Steam Packet Co. She was launched on 5 February 1946, and sailed on her maiden voyage on 26 June that year. However, when the Fleetwood route was closed in 1961 and the new car ferry *Manx Maid* was launched, she became surplus to requirements and was sold to the Chandris Group for service as a cruise ship in the Mediterranean.

She was renamed *Barrow Queen* for the voyage to Piraeus and, on her arrival, she was converted to a luxury cruise ship and became *Carina*. In 1964 she was renamed *Fiesta* and carried out Mediterranean cruises from Greece to Turkey, Cyprus and Israel. *Fiesta* was replaced by a more modern vessel in 1981, and was broken up at Perama.

Argentina Star	1947	**Blue Star Line**	**Nos. 1,173**
Brasil Star	1947	**153m x 21m**	**1,174,**
Uruguay Star	1948	**16 knots**	**1,180**
Paraguay Star	1948	**10,722grt**	**and 1,181.**

Argentina Star, Brasil Star, Uruguay Star and *Paraguay Star* were replacements for five 'A' Class passenger vessels lost during the Second World War. *Argentina Star* and *Brasil Star* were delivered in 1947 and *Uruguay Star* sailed on her maiden voyage from Liverpool on 22 May 1948. On her return, she and her sisters were employed on their owner's London–Buenos Aires service.

In 1950, the ownership of *Argentina Star* and *Brasil Star* was transferred to the Union International Co., with the Blue Star Line remaining as the ship managers. On 12 August 1969, a serious engine room fire damaged *Paraguay Star* while she was berthed at the Royal Victoria Dock in London. It was decided that the ship was beyond economical repair and she was sold to Eckhardt & Co. in Hamburg, where she was broken up.

SS Argentina Star *smoking room. (Courtesy of Wirral Archives Service)*

Corinthic.

Corinthic   **1947**   **Shaw Savill &**   **15,896grt**
                                 171m x 22m   **Albion Line**   **No.1,175**
                                               17 knots

Corinthic was the first of a class of four passenger cargo vessels built for the Shaw Savill Line. The other ships were *Athenic* (1947), *Gothic* (1948) and *Ceramic* (1948), and they all had accommodation for eighty-five first-class passengers.

She was launched on 30 May 1946, and sailed on her maiden voyage from Liverpool–Sydney on 12 April 1947. On her return she was employed on her owner's London–Australia–New Zealand service. Her passenger facilities were removed at Schiedan during an overhaul in 1965. On 23 October 1969 she arrived at Kaohsiung to be broken up.

City of Pretoria   **1947**   **Ellerman &**   **8,450grt**
                                   152m x 20m   **Bucknall Line**   **No.1,176**
                                               15 knots

City of Pretoria was delivered to the Ellerman & Bucknall Line in November 1947, and served on the company's routes from the various British ports to Colombo, Calcutta, Rangoon, East and South Africa and Mauritius.

She was sold to Embajada Cia Nav. Panama in 1967, and was renamed *Proxeneion* for her delivery voyage to the Far East and the shipbreakers at Osaka.

City of Pretoria.

St Patrick.

St Patrick	1948	**Fishguard &**	**3,482grt**
	98m x 15m	**Rosslare Railway**	**No.1,183**
	20 knots	**& Harbour Co.**	

St Patrick and her sister *St David* were both launched at the yard in 1947, and *St Patrick* completed her sea trials on 23 January the following year. She sailed on her maiden voyage from Weymouth–Channel Islands on 4 February, and remained on that service until October each year until 1963. On completion of the season she was laid up at Fishguard every year.

However, on 1 January 1950, the railway port at Fishguard and its ships were transferred to the London Midland Region, and she was then laid up in the winter at Holyhead. Her ownership was transferred to the British Transport Commission, Southern Region, in 1959 and during the winter of 1960/61 she undertook an extensive refurbishment, becoming a one-class vessel on the Channel Islands service.

In 1963 she replaced *Brittany* on the Jersey–St Malo service, which included weekend Weymouth sailings. Later that year, she moved to Southampton to release *Normannia* to be converted to a car ferry. The Weymouth sailings closed in 1964 and the Southampton to Le Havre route was taken over by *Townsend Thoresen*, and she was transferred to the Southampton to St Malo route. Following the final St Malo to Southampton sailing, she sailed for Smiths Dock Co. at South Shields for conversion to a side-loading car ferry.

Pyrrhus.

She was operating on the Folkstone–Boulogne service in 1965 and, was given additional passenger space at Immingham in the winter of 1967. Following an accident at Weymouth involving *Ceasarea* in 1968, the *St Patrick* replaced her while she was repaired. Her final sailing from Boulogne took place on 25 September 1971, and she was laid up at Newhaven. The following year she was sold to Gerasimos S. Fetouris and was renamed *Thermopylae* and, in 1973 she was bought by the Agapitos Brothers at Piraeus and renamed *Agapitos 1* for the Piraeus–Cyclades–Tenos–Mykonos route. She remained on this service until 1976 when she was laid up, and in 1980 she was broken up at Perama.

Pyrrhus	**1949**	**Blue Funnel Line**	**10,093grt**
	157m x 21m	**18½ knots**	**No.1,187**

In November 1964, a serious fire broke out on the *Pyrrhus* while she was unloading cargo at Liverpool. Firefighters took nearly 24 hours to control the blaze, and the ship was at risk of capsizing on several occasions. *Pyrrhus* was repaired and gave the Blue Funnel Line a further eight years' service. She was sold for demolition at Kaohsiung in 1972.

| **City of Liverpool** | 1949 | **Ellerman Hall Line** | 7,612grt |
| | 148m x 19m | 14 knots | No.1,191 |

City of Liverpool was launched at the yard by the Mayoress of Liverpool on 4 November 1948, and sailed on her trials on 3 May the following year. She was the first vessel owned by the line to hold the name, and she sailed on her maiden voyage from the Mersey to Canada, the USA, and the Far East on 6 May.

In 1967 she was sold for £107,000 to Astro Tridente Cia.Nav. S.A. of Panama, and was renamed *Kavo Grossos*. She survived with them for six years and was broken up in Shanghai in 1973.

| **Manchester Spinner** | 1952 | **Manchester Liners** | 7,815grt |
| | 142m x 18m | 15 knots | No.1,217 |

Cammell Laird built *Manchester Spinner* and her sister *Manchester Mariner* in 1952 and 1955 respectively. The *Manchester Spinner* was delivered in July 1952 and was placed on the owner's Atlantic services from the Port of Manchester. On 30 March 1954 she was able to dock at Montreal, creating the record of the earliest opening of the St Lawrence.

She was employed on the Manchester service until 1968 when she was sold to Estia Cia Nav. S.A. of Piraeus, and renamed *Estia*. On 25 November 1971 she experienced an engine room explosion and sank off the coast of Somalia.

Manchester Mariner was sold to Mira Cia Nav. S.A. of Piraeus in 1968, and became *Ira*. She was sold to the National Steel Corporation, Manila, in 1974 and was renamed *Panday Ira*. In October 1975 she suffered a boiler failure at Singapore and was towed to Manila. Following survey and assessment she was declared uneconomical to repair and was broken up at Manila Bay in 1977.

City of Liverpool.

Manchester Spinner.

| **San Fortunato** | 1955 | **Shell Tankers** | 12,278grt |
| | 169m x 21m | 14½ knots | No.1,241 |

Launched as *San Fortunato*, she became *Hemimactra* in 1964. She was broken up in Kaohsiung in 1977.

San Fortunato.

Game Cock V.

Game Cock V 1953 **Liverpool Screw** 218grt
32m x 8m **Towing &** No.1,247
Lighterage
Co. Ltd

She was renamed *Wellington* in 1970 and became *Vernicos Nicos* the following year.

Cheshire Coast 1954 **Coast Lines** 1,202grt
78m x 12m **12 knots** No.1,251

Cheshire Coast was built for Coast Lines services around the British Isles. She was chartered by the Brocklebank Line in 1967 and renamed *Malabar*. She was also chartered by the Prince Line in 1967, and became *Spartan Prince*, reverting to *Cheshire Coast* again in 1971, when she was sold by Coast Lines and was renamed *Venture,* and *Azelia* in 1974. She survived until 1980, when she was sold for breaking up in Cartagena.

Cheshire Coast.

Manxman 1955 **Isle of Man Steam** 2,495 grt
105m x 15m **Packet Co.** No.1,259
21 knots

Manxman was launched on 8 February 1955 and was the fifth vessel of the class to be built by Cammell Laird since the war. She was completed in time for the summer season, and sailed on her maiden voyage from Douglas–Liverpool on 21 May 1955. She served on all of the Steam Packet's routes and worked the winter service with other steamers until the introduction of the passenger car ferries. She grounded in the Mersey in September 1957 but was re-floated with the tide without the aid of tugs. In 1960, the bridge deck was extended to accommodate additional life saving equipment required under new regulations.

On 4 September 1982 she sailed on her last passenger voyage for the Steam Packet from Liverpool–Douglas, and returned later that day. The following day she sailed with passengers to the Albert Edward Dock at Preston to be used as a nightclub. The 'Finished with Engines' cruise was a celebration of the ship's heritage and epitomised a confident hope for her future. However, this hope was short-lived as Marda Squash, the new owners, wanted to give the visitors a sense of nostalgia and she was opened as a visitor attraction. The ship was also available for various functions, but unfortunately the venture was not a success.

She was then converted to a nightclub under the ownership of Mid-nite Entertainments, but she had to leave Preston and was moved to a berth at Waterloo Dock in Liverpool in 1990. *Manxman* was towed to Hull in April 1994 for use as a nightclub, and in 1997 she was moved to Sunderland. While at her berth at Sunderland she began to take on water on 12 June 1999 and was partially submerged.

Between 1997 and 1999 various plans were considered, including a move to Dublin for use as a nightclub, but none of them came to fruition. However, in May 2002 the Manxman Steamship Co. was formed, which aimed to buy, restore and bring her back into public use. The Company was officially incorporated on 3 July and an agreement was drawn up with the owners of the ship that the Manxman Steamship Co. was the preferred buyer of the vessel.

The Steam Packet Co. offered full support for the project and has offered invaluable resources and backing. The profile of the ship as an example of British and Manx maritime heritage has been firmly re-established after years of neglect. In 2003 the *Manxman* Steamship Co. chartered the Isle of Man vessel *Lady of Mann* for an evening cruise around the island with the *Manxman*'s name pennant flying at her mainmast.

The ship has been recognised by the Greenwich Maritime Museum and has been placed on the designated list of vessels of great significance, and a 'Friends of the *Manxman*' support group has been formed. The Heritage Lottery Fund granted the Company £20,000 to fund hull surveys and feasibility studies for the proposed future uses of the vessel, which include a maritime and tourist heritage centre, conference and hospitality suites and hotel facilities for social events.

On 29 September 2003, the *Manxman* left her moorings for the first time since 1997, and was moved the short distance to the interior dock of the Pallion yard for preliminary work to begin. The tugs guided her inch by inch perfectly through the dock gates and she settled on the blocks a few hours later.

Manxman.

Manxman.

A further boost to the Company came when charitable status was finally granted to the Manxman Steamship Co., which should open up further funding opportunities with the favourable tax concessions available to registered charities. The Company has achieved much in a relatively short time but much needs to be done as there is a long way to go before the ship is back in pristine Steam Packet condition.

The vessel represents a very important part of the commercial and maritime history of the United Kingdom and recalls a period in Britain's maritime history when steamers were a common sight and the Isle of Man Steam Packet vessels formed a vital link for the community from the Isle of Man to the mainland. *Manxman* is the sole survivor of the classic turbine passenger type that served on Britain's short sea ferry routes for many years.

City of Wellington	**1956**	**Ellerman Hall**	**7,702grt**
	155m x 21m	**Line**	**No.1,245**
		15 knots	

City of Wellington, *City of Newcastle* and *City of Winnipeg* were delivered to the Ellerman Hall Line in 1956. *City of Newcastle* was built by Alexander Stephen & Sons at Glasgow, and *City of Winnipeg* by the Caledon Shipbuilding and Engineering Co. at Dundee.

City of Wellington was sold to Mulroy Bay Shipping Co. of Liberia, renamed *Eastern Enterprise* and sold to the shipbreakers at Kaohsiung, where she arrived on 15 February 1979.

Her sister, *City of Newcastle*, was chartered to the Ben Line in 1968, and became *Benratha*. On completion of the charter in 1970, she became *City of Wellington* again, managed

City of Wellington.

by Ellerman & Bucknall. She was sold in 1978 to the Gulf East Ship Management Ltd, and was renamed *Eastern Envoy*. She resold again that year, retaining the same name. On 23 October 1980 she arrived at Chittagong to be broken up.

City of Winnipeg was also chartered to the Ben Line in 1968, becoming *Benedin*, and was transferred back to Ellerman & Bucknall in 1970 and renamed *City of Delhi*. In 1976 she was sold to Beaumaris Shipping and was renamed *Fexl Glory*, and was broken up at Chittagong in 1980.

Carnatic.

Carnatic	1957	**Shaw Savill &**	**11,144grt**
	156m x 21m	**Albion Line**	**No.1,269**
		17 knots	

Carnatic was the fifth and last of the 'C' Class. She was launched by Mrs W. Donald, and sailed on her maiden voyage from Liverpool–Auckland in February 1957. She remained on the Line's services until 1973, when she was transferred to Royal Mail Line management and renamed *Darro*, employed on their service to South American ports.

She was sold in 1977 and renamed *Litska K*, and *Dimitra* in 1979, when she was broken up.

| **Sepia** | 1961 | **Shell Tankers** | **42,109grt** |
| | **249m x 34m** | **16 knots** | **No.1,278** |

At the time of her launch, *Sepia* was the largest and longest tanker built by Cammell Laird. She was built for Shell Tankers N.V. of Rotterdam, and was launched by Mrs Wilkinson, the wife of the Managing Director of the Royal Dutch Shell Group. *Sepia* was the first the yard had built for Shell Tankers N.V. of Rotterdam, but was the twelfth they had built since they commenced building for the Shell Group.

Accommodation was provided in the poop for seamen and engine room ratings and, in addition, the refrigerated chambers and sundry storerooms were arranged at the after end. The navigating officers were accommodated on the bridge deck, amidships of the captain's accommodation, together with that for the pilot, owner's room and lounge. All the crew accommodation was ventilated, air cooled and heated by mechanical means.

Sepia.

The oil-carrying compartments consisted of fourteen main tanks, each sub-divided by longitudinal bulkheads into three compartments. The peak tank forward was a dry tank and the after peak tank was arranged for water ballast. The propelling machinery consisted of one high-pressure and one low-pressure ahead turbines, also one high-pressure and one low-pressure astern turbines.

In April 1975 *Sepia* arrived at Brunei Bay, south of Labuan, at the eastern side of the South China Sea, to lay up due to the depressed state of the price of oil. In 1977 she was used to lighten tankers off the Mississippi entrance, unloading oil from tankers for delivery to Garyville Refinery on the river. She had been laid up at Labuan with her sister *Serenia*, which was moved in 1977 for North Sea work. *Sepia* was sold for scrapping at Kaohsiung, where she arrived on 30 August 1983.

Ionic	**1959**	**Shaw Savill Line**	**11,219grt**
	156m x 21m	**17 knots**	**No.1,281**

Ionic was launched by Mrs D.W. Donaldson and was the first of a class of 'I' ships — the others were *Illyric*, *Icenic* and *Iberic*. They were all single-screw driven motorships, powered by a single turbo-charged diesel engine. This power unit gave the vessels a service speed of 17 knots on a continuous output on eight cylinders at 11,500bhp, with a reserve of power up to 13,300bhp. The vessel was built to Lloyds Class 100A1, with four refrigerated holds and two general cargo holds and corresponding tween decks. There were a total of twenty-three spaces for the carriage of frozen meat, chilled beef, fruit and dairy products.

On her maiden voyage from Liverpool she carried a great variety of goods for discharge in New Zealand. Among her cargo was 1,200 tons of salt, 400 tons of various sodas, 400 tons of cased motor cars, 1,200 tons of steel, 3,500 cases of Scotch whisky and two fully assembled electric locomotives of 40 tons each for New Zealand Railways. She also carried a propeller that was stowed on her after deck that was
made by Manganese Bronze and Brass Co. at Birkenhead. This was held in reserve at Wellington for any of the Company's ships of the *Ionic* Class that may have need of a new propeller while in the vicinity of New Zealand.

Ionic and her sisters were specially designed for Shaw Savill's service from the United Kingdom–Australia and New Zealand via Suez, Panama or the Cape. She was sold in 1978 and became *Glenparva*, and was sold to be broken up in 1979.

Cheshire	**1959**	**Bibby Line**	**7,201grt**
	137m x 19m	**17 knots**	**No.1,283**

Cheshire was launched at the yard on 23 April 1959 by Lady Bibby, and sailed on her maiden voyage from Birkenhead–Burma on 10 October that year. *Cheshire*, *Shropshire* and *Yorkshire* were three similar sister ships built mainly for the charter trade, and which spent most of their lives on services other than the core Bibby Line routes.

Cheshire was the third vessel of that name in the history of the Bibby Line and was designed as an open shelter deck type, but with scantlings arranged for deeper draft should the owners decide to close the shelter deck. All accommodation was situated amidships and a complete system of air-conditioning was installed. Propelling machinery consisted of

Ionic.

Cheshire.

a Fairfield Doxford two-stroke cycle, six-cylinder, opposed piston oil engine, developing 8,100 bhp at 120rpm, and the main engine was designed to operate on heavy fuel.

She was sold to Messageries Maritimes in 1968 and was renamed *Mozambique* for the African and Madagascar service. In April 1970 she assisted in the rescue of crew from the tanker *Silver Cloud*, which had broken into two pieces following an explosion. In September 1974 she was in Mozambique when she assisted in the evacuation of civilians caught in hostilities during the Civil War.

In 1976 she was renamed *Kota Mewah* following her sale to Pacific International Lines of Singapore, and arrived at Kaohsiung on 24 August 1984 to be broken up.

Her sister, *Shropshire*, was sold by the Bibby Line in 1972 to Lefkonia Cia Naviera S.A., Panama, and renamed *Argiro,* then *Naftilos* in 1984, and broken up at Chittagong in 1985. *Yorkshire* was sold in 1971 and renamed *Bordabekoa*, then *Sea Reliance* in 1981, and was broken up at Bombay in 1984.

Left: *Cammell Laird / Bibby Line brochure, published in 1959.*

Below: *HMS* Devonshire *leaves the Mersey for trials in 1962.*

| **HMS Devonshire** | 1962 | **Royal Navy** | 5,440grt |
| | **158m x 16m** | **31½ knots** | **No.1,284** |

Devonshire was launched at the yard by Her Royal Highness, Princess Alexandra, who was presented with a bouquet by five-year-old Susan Johnson, daughter of Mr R.W. Johnson, chairman and Managing Director of Cammell Laird. She was a County Class destroyer and joined her sisters, *Hampshire, Kent* and *London.*

The class was designed with three main roles: they would perform escort duties with a task group, including the ability to provide guided weapon anti-aircraft defence for the group and to augment its anti-submarine capability; they would be involved in offensive operations as part of the task group of light forces with the ability to bombard in support of land forces, and to attack light forces with gunfire; and they would also participate in police duties in peacetime in any part of the world. Her crew consisted of 33 officers and 438 sailors.

Devonshire carried one 'Seaslug' guided weapons system mounted on the quarter deck, four radar controlled 4.5in guns forward and two 'Seacat' close-range guided weapons systems fitted abaft the after funnel. The ship was also fitted with the latest underwater detection equipment for anti-submarine duties. A Westland Wessex helicopter was also carried on the ship.

In a series of firings from HMS *Girdleness* in 1961, 90 per cent of the 'Seaslug' missiles intercepted the target, and the most outstanding feature of the missile was its degree of reliability. It was also subject to the most rigorous environmental tests including extremes of temperature, damp and vibration. Consequently, it was claimed that 'Seaslug' was the best shipborne surface to air missile in the world at that time. *Devonshire* was also fitted with the latest air and surface warning radars and her operations room was similar to those installed in the aircraft carriers *Victorious* and *Hermes.*

The Yarrow Admiralty Research Department, Associated Electrical Industries Ltd and the ship and engine builders developed the propulsion system. The majority of the propelling machinery was designed and made at A.E.I.'s Trafford Park works. She was built with a pair of geared steam turbines driving one of the ship's propeller shafts which provided the main source of power at normal speeds. There was also an additional pair of 7,500hp-gas turbines connected through gearing to one of the shafts. Consequently, *Devonshire* could leave port almost immediately in an emergency without raising steam, as the gas turbines could reach full power very rapidly when starting from cold. Steam was then raised and the turbines could then be brought into use.

She was also fitted with stabilisers which were useful when the helicopter was operating in bad weather conditions. She was commissioned in November 1962 at a service at the yard when the Chaplain of the Fleet, The Venerable John Armstrong, blessed the ship. The service was conducted in the presence of the Chief of Defence Staff, Admiral of the Fleet Earl Mountbatten of Burma.

Devonshire completed her first commission to the United States in 1963 and, when she visited Philadelphia the ship's company was presented with the freedom of the city. This was followed by visits to the West Indies and Mediterranean ports, including Malta. She completed commissions around the world and in 1976 she visited Odessa and Constanta, which was followed by an official visit to Haifa. *Devonshire* was paid off in 1978 and was sunk in 1984, when she was used for target practice.

Windsor Castle	1960	**Union Castle**	**37,640grt**
	238m x 28m	**Line**	**No.1,287**
	22½ knots		

HM Queen Elizabeth the Queen Mother launched *Windsor Castle* on 23 June 1959. The Cammell Laird publication of the launch said:

> It was a day to remember; a day on which the sun shone unceasingly, and a gracious lady came to launch a magnificent ship. From the arrival of Her Majesty, to the moment when the *Windsor Castle* came quietly alongside the wall of the fitting-out basin, everything went smoothly and with perfect precision.

At the time of her launch she was the largest liner built in England, the largest liner owned by the Line and the first Union Castle liner built by Cammell Laird.

She sailed on her maiden voyage from Southampton–Cape Town and Durban on 18 August 1960. She was designed to carry 191 first-class and 591 tourist-class passengers, and 475 crew. She was also designed with extensive cargo spaces which were carried in seven holds and associated tween decks, three of which were forward of the main machinery space, and four aft. Nos 1, 2, 7 and 8 holds were for general cargo and the remaining and tween decks for refrigerated cargos of fruit. Several of the refrigerated spaces were suitable for chilled meat and frozen produce, and a number of the chambers were arranged for deep-freeze cargos.

The ship's propelling machinery consisted of a two-shaft arrangement of compound condensing double-reduction geared turbines which were capable of developing 10 per cent continuous overload power in excess of normal service power. Her three boilers of Babcock & Wilcox selectable superheat design were manufactured by Cammell Laird.

She served on the Union Castle Line mailship service until 1977, when she made her last passenger sailing from Southampton on 12 August. It was her 124th sailing and she arrived back at Southampton on 19 September for the last time. She was sold to John Latsis at Piraeus and sailed from Southampton on 3 October 1977 for Greece. She was renamed *Margarita L* and was refitted as an 852-berth luxury accommodation ship. She was initially used as an office and leisure centre for the Latsis-owned Petrola International S.A. Construction Co. at Rabegh. In February 1979 she replaced the ex-Elder Dempster Liner *Aureol* which was renamed *Marianna VI*, at a special jetty two miles north of Jeddah, Saudi Arabia, as the centre of a complex of car parks, swimming pools and sports facilities.

A helicopter pad was added to her former first-class promenade deck pool area, and she returned to Greece for overhaul in 1983. She was towed to Eleusis Bay in Greece in 1990, and laid up with occasional private use by Mr Latsis, but was offered for sale in 1998.

The RMS *Windsor Castle* Preservation Society was formed in 2003, with the aim of raising funds, interest and support to bring the vessel back to Britain to be used as a museum/education centre, incorporating restaurants, a conference centre and tourist attractions. It has been suggested that the ship be permanently berthed at Southampton, Plymouth, Falmouth, Liverpool or London, and various studies are in progress to ascertain the feasibility of the project.

Windsor Castle.

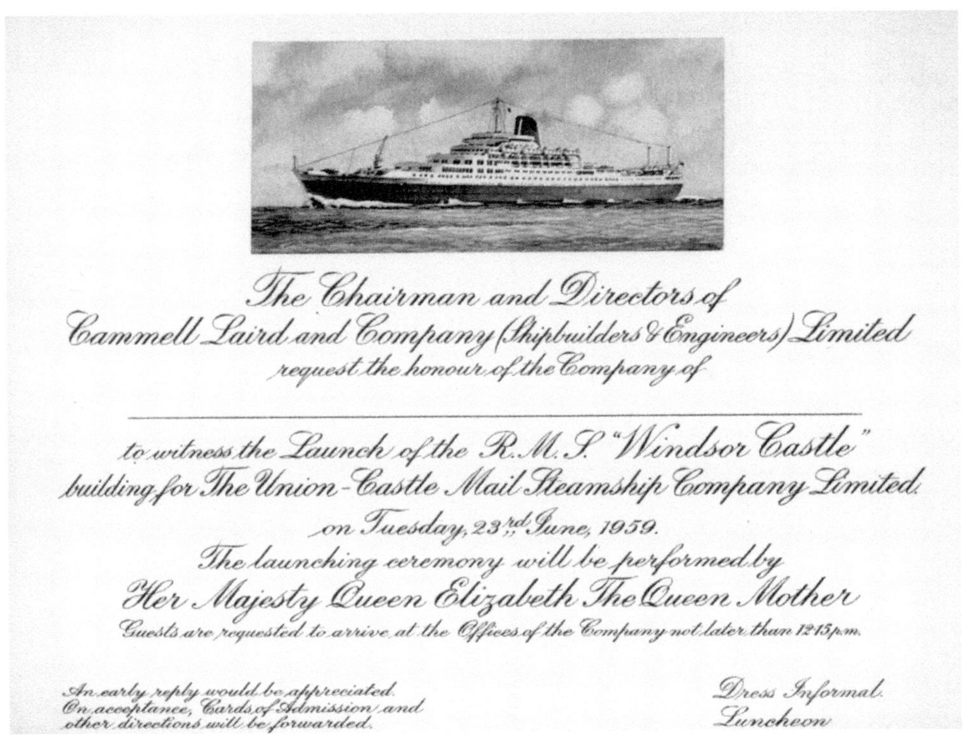

Launch ticket for Windsor Castle.

Left to right: West Cock, Heath Cock, Weather Cock.

West Cock	**1958**	**192grt**	**Liverpool Screw Towing Co. Ltd**
Heath Cock	**1958**	**193grt**	**Liverpool Screw Towing Co. Ltd**
Weather Cock	**1960**	**159grt**	**Liverpool Screw Towing Co. Ltd** **Nos 1295, 1296 and 1300**

These were three examples of Mersey tugs that were built by the yard to assist ships to manoeuvre in the river and the dock system. The Liverpool Screw Towing Co. was absorbed into the fleet of the Alexandra Towing Co. *Weather Cock* became *Formby* in 1970 and *Vernicos Alexia* in 1981; *West Cock* was renamed *Morpeth* in 1970 and *Vernicos Giannis* in 1982; *Heath Cock* was renamed *Collingwood* in 1970, and *Collingwood II* and *Vernicos Barbara IV* in 1981.

Vernicos Alexia and *Vernicos Barbara IV*, owned by Nicholas E. Vernicos Shipping Co. of Greece, were being towed from the Mersey to Piraeus by the *Vernicos Giorgis* (ex-*Pea Cock*) and became stranded west of Solva, South Wales, on 18 October 1981, after her propeller became fouled in bad weather. The St David's lifeboat and a helicopter rescued her crew of eight. The three tugs were driven aground and were later declared a total loss.

Vernicos Giannis sank off Iraklion on 9 August 1983, after being in collision with the *Atalante*. She was refloated on 20 October and, while being towed, she was lost off Falconera, in the Cyclades, after breaking adrift in rough weather.

Oscilla.

Oscilla   1963   Shell Tankers Ltd   228m x 31m
16 knots   No.1289

Oscilla was launched on 12 October 1962 by Lady Caccia. *Oscilla* was designed to carry petroleum in bulk, with a curved raked stem, falling out cruiser stern with after superstructure and forecastle.

All accommodation was situated aft with the captain's and owner's accommodation on the boat deck, and a combined wheelhouse and chart-room, radio room and gyro/radar room on the navigation bridge deck. The hull was sub-divided into fore peak, oil fuel deep tank and pump room, cofferdam, twelve sets of cargo and ballast compartments, pump room and bunker tanks and machinery space with double bottom and after peak.

She was propelled by a single screw driven by a geared steam turbine installation of Pametrada design and Cammell Laird manufacture, developing 16,000shp at about 106rpm when supplied with steam.

Arkadia.

Arkadia

The Greek Line passenger vessel *Arkadia* (20,259grt/1931) in Grayson Rollo's No.1 Drydock. The picture also shows Woodside Mainline station and Woodside bus terminal. The dock was officially opened by the Birkenhead ferry *Woodchurch* on 8 October 1960. Grayson Rollo merged with Cammell Laird in 1962.

Serenia.

Serenia

The Shell tanker *Serenia* (42,082 grt/1961) in Grayson Rollo & Clover's newly enlarged No.1 Dock in 1961. The overhang of the bow allowed the 249m-vessel to enter the 244m-long dock. *Serenia* was laid up at Labuan in 1975, and was moved in 1977 for North Sea work. She was converted by Rhine–Schelde–Verolme at Rotterdam for offshore oil loading, and was employed in the North Sea until 1987, when Shell purchased the Norwegian tanker *Gerina* (65,173grt/1980) to replace her. She left the Mersey on 10 July and arrived at Kaohsiung on 4 September 1987 to be broken up.

Retriever	**1961**	**Cable & Wireless Ltd**	
4,000grt			
	101m x 15m	**15 knots**	**No.1302**

Cable Ship *Retriever* was the first ship designed and constructed for the recovery and overboarding of new coaxial-type telephone cables with submerged repeaters inserted for Cable & Wireless Ltd. She had an operating range of 8,000 miles, a maximum speed of 15 knots, a sea endurance of seven weeks and a cable capacity of 21,000 cu.ft., which is equivalent to 420 miles of conventional deep-sea cable, in three tanks. The captain's, officer's and crew accommodation, testing rooms, radio office, hospital, surgery, lounge and dining room were all air-conditioned.

Retriever was designed to be the first Cable & Wireless vessel to be based at Suva, which is one of the landing points of the trans-Pacific section of the Commonwealth round-the-world telephone cable. While there, the ship would be available to give any help in the laying and maintenance of the cable.

She had a large hold and tween deck arranged forward for the stowage of cable equipment,

Retriever.

which was served by two 5-ton derricks mounted on the bridge front. She was designed to handle cable forward and aft using the forward cable machinery in each case. When the cable was repaired at the bow it passed over large diameter sheaves fitted at the extreme forward end of the vessel. Only certain types of cable could be handled over the chute built into the after end of the ship.

Retriever was propelled by diesel electric machinery manufactured by the English Electric Co. that comprised a four-engine arrangement, each engine driving a d.c. main propulsion electric generator. The vessel was designed to be completely controlled from the bridge, and also from a position at the forward end of the upper deck. The bow control position was in operation when the vessel was on cable operations. *Retriever* sailed from Hong Kong on her final voyage to Alang, where she arrived on 17 April 1995 to be broken up.

Manx Maid	1962 105m x 16m	**Isle of Man Steam Packet Co.** 21 knots	2,724grt No.1,303

Manx Maid was the Isle of Man's first car ferry and was specially designed by Cammell Laird with a series of ramps which allowed vehicles to be unloaded and loaded at all stages of the tide at Douglas. Prior to her entry in service, vehicles had been lifted on and off the vessels by crane. She was launched on 23 January 1962 by Mrs A. Alexander, the wife of a director of the Isle of Man Steam Packet Co., and sailed on her maiden voyage on 23 May from Liverpool to Douglas.

She was able to carry 80 cars and 1,400 passengers in two classes, and was also the first Isle of Man Steam Packet ship to be fitted with anti-roll stabilisers. The public rooms for first-class passengers included a general and ladies' saloon on the lower deck and a dining saloon on the promenade deck. She was propelled by twin screws driven by two sets of Pametrada turbines through double-reduction gearing. Each set comprised a single ahead turbine of the impulse type and one impulse astern turbine incorporated in the ahead turbine casing.

Manx Maid collided with the Fort Anne jetty in rough weather in November 1974, and was sent to Birkenhead to enter the drydock for inspection and repair. Unfortunately, she was then involved in an industrial dispute but returned to service in time for the busy T.T. sailings.

Manx Maid was so successful that a sister ship was ordered from Cammell Laird and *Ben-My-Chree* entered service on 12 May 1966. She was similar to *Manx Maid* and was the last Isle of Man vessel to enter service as a two-class ship, and became a one-class vessel the following year.

The Steam Packet sold *Manx Maid* to Devascus Ltd for static use as a nightclub at Bristol, and she had her stabilisers removed to be fitted to the new *Mona's Isle*. She left Birkenhead under tow for Bristol on 10 April 1985. As the owners failed to obtain planning permission at Bristol, *Manx Maid* was sold to the shipbreakers at Garston and she left Avonmouth for the Mersey on 8 February 1986.

Ben-My-Chree was sold to the New England Development Co. in 1985 to become a restaurant ship at Jacksonville in Florida. However, she was again needed on the Manx routes and was chartered from her new owners between 25 May and 9 June that year. The ambitious plans to sail *Ben-My-Chree* across the Atlantic to Florida did not materialise and she lay in Vittoria Dock at Birkenhead until she was sold to the shipbreakers at Santander in 1989.

Manx Maid *in the river Mersey in 1966.*

Builders' cut-out view of Manx Maid.

TELEPHONE: 7080 BIRKENHEAD   TELEX 62463.   TELEGRAMS: CAMELLAIRD, BIRKENHEAD

MERSEY RAILWAY: GREEN LANE STATION

CAMMELL LAIRD & CO. (SHIPBUILDERS & ENGINEERS) LIMITED.

Shipbuilding & Engineering Works

Birkenhead

26th November, 1965.

IN YOUR REPLY PLEASE REFER TO

WJS/EC

I. Collard, Esq.,
3, Churchill Avenue,
BIRKENHEAD.

Dear Sir,

We now have pleasure in enclosing 2 permits for the launching of the "Ben-my-Chree" on Friday, 10th December, 1965, at 11.30 a.m. and would draw your attention to the conditions printed on the back of the permit.

Yours faithfully,

FOR AND ON BEHALF OF
CAMMELL LAIRD & COMPANY
(Shipbuilders & Engineers) LIMITED.

E. H. DODD Manager Commercial Services

Letter from Cammell Laird Co. Ltd enclosing tickets for the launch of Ben-My-Chree *on Friday 10 December 1965.*

Overchurch.

Overchurch	1962	**Birkenhead**	468grt
	47m x 10m	Corporation	No.1,304
			12 knots

Overchurch was ordered by Birkenhead Corporation in 1960 as the third new vessel for the Birkenhead (Woodside) to Liverpool (Pier Head) service. Philip & Son Ltd of Dartmouth, Devon, delivered *Mountwood* and *Woodchurch*. They were the first diesel ships to join the fleet and were powered by two 8-cylinder engines manufactured by Crosley Brothers of Manchester, which drive twin screws and develop 1,400bhp in total. The engines are fitted with special air brakes and a servo. The third sister, *Overchurch*, was the first ferry built for Birkenhead Corporation that was all welded and one of the main differences in design is that she had the wheelhouse across the breadth of the ship.

The Mersey ferries can be traced back to a service provided by Benedictine monks in 1150. In 1330 King Edward III granted a licence to operate a ferry across the river. Over the centuries, ownership of the ferry service changed regularly and, in 1822, a steam-driven ferry was provided, along with the introduction of a wooden paddle steamer. The Woodside, Eastham, Egremont, Seacombe and New Brighton services came under the control of local government boards and remained under Birkenhead and Wallasey Corporation control until the services were given to the Merseyside Passenger Transport Authority, following the 1968 Transport Act and local government reorganisation in 1974.

Woodchurch was taken out of service in 1981 and was laid up for over three years, but was brought back into service in 1983. In 1984 the International Garden Festival took place on the banks of the Mersey. The ferries provided a new service to Otterspool and were painted in a new livery of red, white and blue. In 1989 *Woodchurch* and *Mountwood* were given major refits and their bridges were rebuilt, and *Overchurch* was left to operate a triangular service from Liverpool–Seacombe and Woodside. *Overchurch* was given a major refit by Lengthline Ship Repairers at Manchester in 1998, and was renamed *Royal Daffodil*.

The Mersey ferry is now mainly a leisure service providing cruises alongside the triangular service but also reverts back to the traditional ferry service in the morning and evening rush hours. *Mountwood* was given the name *Royal Iris of the Mersey* in 2002 and early in 2004 *Woodchurch* entered A&P's yard at Birkenhead to be refitted and re-engined, and entered service in July that year, later being renamed *Snowdrop*.

Mercury	1962	**Cable &**	8,000grt
	144m x 18m	**Wireless Ltd**	No.1,305
		16 knots	

At the time of her launch *Mercury* was the world's fastest and most modern cable-layer. Lady Joan Macpherson, the wife of Sir John Macpherson, chairman of Cable & Wireless Ltd, launched her at the yard on 20 July 1962.

She was a cable laying and cable repair vessel, and was designed and built to Lloyds Class 100A1. For cable ships the steel structure is almost entirely welded, seams and butts of the shell being flush and the hull was specially strengthened for navigation on ice.

A cellular double bottom was fitted throughout, forming water ballast fresh water and oil tanks. Oil fuel bunkers were fitted forward of the motor room and the capacity of the tanks were designed to give the vessel sixty days' supply of fuel and water while continuously at sea.

Mercury.

Special consideration was given to the trim of the vessel when laying cables and to obtain the best balance possible, the diesel engine room was aft of the midships and the electric propulsion motor room was as far aft as possible, while three cable tanks were fitted forward of the engine and propulsion motor rooms. The coiling capacity of the cable tanks was over 99,000 cu.ft, which is equivalent to approximately 1,200 miles of lightweight cable.

The cable machinery was arranged on the upper and bridge decks, and the forward cable machinery was forward of the bridge front for picking up cable for repair and laying armoured cable in shallow water at speeds of up to 8 knots, and could withstand a pull of 30 tons. The after cable machinery was capable of paying out cable at 8 knots and sustaining a load of 6 tons. *Mercury* was powered by diesel-electric machinery manufactured by English Electric, which developed a total service power of 6,000shp at around 146rpm.

While she was berthed at Bristol, *Mercury* suffered a fire in her engine room on 1 May 1996. She was sold to shipbreakers in Spain and arrived at Gijon in tow from Bristol on 3 December 1997.

Wirral Coast	1962	**Coast Lines**	**881grt**
	57m x 11m	12 knots	No.1,308

Wirral Coast was built at the yard for services around the coast of the British Isles and to Ireland. She was designed to carry trailers or containers in the hold and containers on top of the MacGregor hatch covers. Her bipod masts had 6-ton derricks situated forward and aft, which were suitable for handling general cargo, but quay facilities were required to unload the containers and trailers. She was designed as a very versatile and specialist ship, as she was built to accept general cargo carried conventionally. She was fitted with a

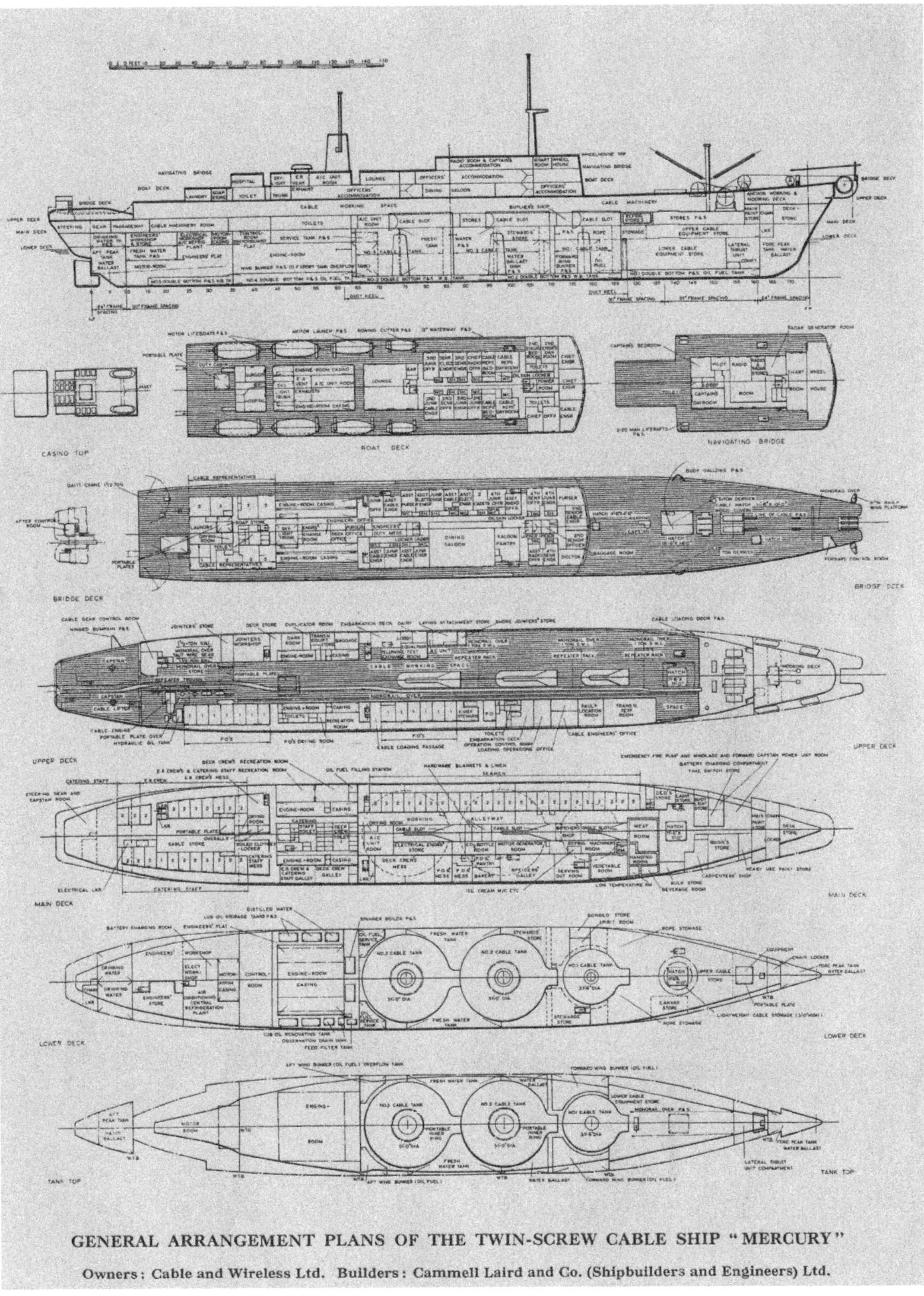

General arrangement plans of the twin-screw cable ship Mercury.

Wirral Coast.

6-cylinder single-acting two-stroke Sulzer engine, developing 1,200bhp at around 235rpm, and ran on standard diesel fuel.

At the launch in July 1962 by Mrs Hill, the wife of the secretary of the Liverpool Steamship Owners Association, Mr R.W. Johnson, chairman and Managing Director of Cammell Laird, said that the facilities offered by *Wirral Coast* would help to provide an answer to the problems of road and rail congestion. Mr Arnet Robinson, vice-chairman and Managing Director of Coast Lines, said that they maintained confidence in providing and modernising the fleet, even though the competition with land routes was very intense and, if this situation continued, some services would have to be withdrawn.

Wirral Coast survived for only ten years in this financial climate and, in 1972, she was sold to Usborne & Sons and was renamed *Shevrell*. She was sold again in 1974, becoming *Portmarnock*, *Nadia 1* in 1979. She sank at Khalde on 27 November 1985, and was abandoned as a total loss.

Arkadia and Queen of Bermuda

In the early 1960s two famous liners arrived on Merseyside for their annual overhauls. They were the *Arkadia* and *Queen of Bermuda* which had been built as sister ships by Vickers Armstrong on the Tyne and at Barrow-in-Furness respectively.

Arkadia was launched on 17 March 1931 as *Monarch of Bermuda* for Furness Withy & Co.'s service from New York–Hamilton, Bermuda. She sailed on the positioning voyage from Liverpool–New York on 21 February 1933 and, on arrival, she sailed each Saturday at 3.00 p.m., arriving at Bermuda at 9.00 a.m. the following Monday. The ship left Bermuda on Wednesday, arriving back at New York at 8.00 a.m. on Friday.

On 8 September 1934 the *Monarch of Bermuda* rescued seventy-nine passengers from the burning passenger liner *Morro Castle* and, in 1937, her registry was changed from

Arkadia *arrives in the Mersey.*

Monarch of Bermuda *and* Queen of Bermuda *at New York. (Painting by Stephen J. Card, H.H. Outerbridge Collection)*

Bermuda to London. At the beginning of the Second World War she was laid up at New York, and in October 1939 she sailed to Liverpool to be converted to a troop-ship. In 1940 she was involved in the Norwegian Campaign and carried part of Britain's gold reserves to North America. She was converted to a Landing Ship Infantry in 1942 and transported 4,000 men to North Africa as part of Operation 'Torch', and carried troops for the landing in Sicily.

At the end of the war she was sent back to her builders on the Tyne to be converted back to a passenger liner, and on 24 March 1947 she was almost destroyed by fire. *Monarch of Bermuda* was sent to the Firth of Forth where a survey was carried out which concluded that her hull and machinery were in good condition. The Ministry of Transport bought her and she was sent to Thornycroft at Southampton and rebuilt as an emigrant carrier to carry 1,600 passengers in one class, and was renamed *New Australia*.

Shaw Savill & Albion Line managed the vessel and she sailed to Sydney on 15 August 1950 with emigrants under the British–Australian Migrant Agreement. In 1953 she also carried troops to Korea. In January 1958 she was sold to the Greek Line, refitted by Blohm & Voss at Hamburg and renamed *Arkadia*, and took her first sailing from Bremerhaven to Quebec and Montreal on 22 May that year. Her accommodation was further modernised in 1961 at Hamburg, and in 1966 she was sold to shipbreakers at Valencia, where she arrived on 18 December.

Her sister, *Queen of Bermuda*, was launched at Vickers Armstrong on 1 September 1932, and sailed on her maiden voyage from Liverpool–New York on 21 February 1933. She then joined the *Monarch of Bermuda* on the New York–Bermuda service. In 1937 her registry was also changed from Bermuda to London, and in 1939 she was taken over and converted into an armed merchant cruiser.

Queen of Bermuda was fitted with seven 6in guns and anti-aircraft weapons, and in 1940 her third funnel was removed. She was converted to a troop-ship in 1943 and carried over 97,000 troops during the remainder of the war. In 1947 she was refitted

Queen of Bermuda *sails from the Mersey in December, 1963.*

for peacetime use and had her third funnel replaced, and three new boilers replaced the original eight.

She was sent to Harland & Wolff at Belfast for her annual overhaul in 1961 and was rebuilt with one funnel. Following successful sea trials on 23 February 1962 she returned to the New York–Bermuda service. On 23 November 1963 she returned to Cammell Laird for her annual refit, which took five weeks to complete. Furness Withy closed the passenger service in 1966 and *Queen of Bermuda* was sold to Shipbreaking Industries Ltd to be broken up at Faslane, where she arrived on 6 December.

| **Scythia** | 1964 | **Cunard Line** | 5,837grt |
| | 139m x 18m | 17½ knots | No.1,314 |

Scythia was built for the North Western Line (Mersey) Ltd, which was a subsidiary set up by Cammell Laird, and she was placed on long-term charter to the Cunard Steamship Co. She was a near sister to *Media*, *Parthia*, *Saxonia* and *Ivernia* which had entered service in 1963 and 1964 for the Cunard Line.

At the launch of *Scythia*, Mr Robert Johnson, chairman and Managing Director of Cammell Laird, reminded the guests that the last time they stood on a platform with a party from the Cunard Line was in July 1938 at the launch of the *Mauretania*. *Scythia* was the first of three vessels built for Cunard Line's 'new-look' cargo fleet on the North Atlantic. Although similar to the 'Media' Class, the *Scythia*, *Samaria* and *Scotia* were slightly larger and faster, and carried about 7,500 tons deadweight of cargo, partly in refrigerated space. The main Sulzer diesel engine was a larger version of that fitted in 'Media', providing a speed of 18 knots.

The sisters were all built to Lloyds highest Class of registry under special survey and to the Ministry of Transport's latest regulations, the International Convention for the Safety of Life at Sea, the Factory Acts and the Manchester Ship Canal regulations.

Scythia.

They were open shelter deck-type with forecastle and after deckhouse. The accommodation and machinery space was situated aft and there were four holds. A third deck was fitted in way of Nos 2, 3, and 4 holds. The double bottom extended fore and aft to carry oil fuel and water ballast clear of the machinery space. Cunard Line naval architects carried out extensive market research while designing this class, resulting in ship's crews, stevedores and shore staff in Liverpool, London and American ports describing them as 'dream ships'. Accommodation for officers and crew was situated in a single deckhouse aft. Plastic-faced panelling and bulk heading was used throughout, and all accommodation was air-conditioned, with most of the crew having their own cabins.

Scythia was launched at the yard on 25 August 1964, and she sailed on her maiden voyage from London–New York later that year. She remained on the Cunard Line's Atlantic services and, with the introduction of larger container vessels on the route, she was purchased by the Cunard Line and sold with her sister *Samaria* in 1969. She became *Merchant*, owned by Thos. & Jas. Harrison, and was used on their United Kingdom–West Indies trade. *Merchant* served with them until 1979, when she was sold to the Totnes Shipping Corporation of Monrovia and renamed *Sisal Trader*.

At the beginning of April 1984 she was driven ashore on Mayotte Island, Madagascar, by cyclone 'Kamisy'. She was refloated on 16 April and sold for scrapping and towed to Gadani Beach to be broken up.

Samaria *(left) – yard No. 1318 – and* Scotia *(opposite above) – yard No. 1324 – were built as sister ships to* Scythia *by Cammell Laird in 1964 and 1966 respectively.*

Scotia.

Ocean Monarch.

| **Ocean Monarch** | **1951** | **Furness Withy** | **13,654grt** |
| | **157m x 22m** | **Line** | **18 knots** |

Ocean Monarch arrived at Cammell Laird's No.5 Drydock on 2 October 1965 for her annual refit. This was her first visit to the yard although another Furness Withy passenger liner, *Queen of Bermuda*, underwent her 1963 and 1964 annual refits at Birkenhead. The refit provided work for about 300 men and lasted for four weeks.

She was launched on 27 July 1950 at Vickers Armstrong yard on the Tyne, and sailed on her maiden voyage from London to New York on 18 April that year. Her first voyage from New York to Bermuda commenced on 3 May, carrying 440 first-class passengers. She was given a major refit in 1961 when her tonnage was re-listed as 13,581grt. *Ocean Monarch* remained on that service, with occasional calls at Nassau, until 1966 when she was withdrawn and laid up on the river Fal.

She was sold to the Bulgarian Shipping Co. in 1967 to be used as a cruise ship in the Mediterranean and Black Sea, and was renamed *Varna*. She also operated to the St Lawrence between 1970 and 1972 with cruises from Montreal, and from Nice in 1973. Following the sudden increase in oil prices she was laid up for several years, and in 1979 she was refitted for use in the Mediterranean and renamed *Riviera*, but this service never materialised and it was rumoured that she was to be chartered by World Cruise Lines for the New York– Bermuda service.

It was also thought that she would be renamed *Venus* for cruising from New York and Florida but she was, in fact, renamed *Reina Del Mar* in 1981 for a proposed service to Scandinavia and the North Cape in the summer, and the Mediterranean in the winter. However, while undergoing a refit on 28 May 1981 she suffered a serious fire at Perama and later capsized. She was declared a total loss.

| **Ocean Monarch** | **1957** | **Shaw Savill &** | **25,585grt** |
| | **195m x 26m** | **Albion Line** | **20 knots** |

Vickers Armstrong Ltd at Walker-on-Tyne built *Ocean Monarch* as *Empress of England* for the Canadian Pacific Steamships Co. and she was launched by Lady Eden, the wife of the British Prime Minister, on 9 May 1956. She was an almost identical sister ship to the *Empress of Britain* which was built by the Fairfield Shipbuilding & Engineering Co., Govan, the previous year.

Ocean Monarch.

The *Empress of England* sailed on her maiden voyage from Liverpool–Quebec and Montreal on 18 April 1957, when she replaced the *Empress of Scotland*. In 1962 she broke adrift in Gladstone Dock at Liverpool, and collided with the Hindustan. Both ships were damaged in the collision. In 1963 she was chartered by the Travel Savings Association, and sailed on her first cruise for them on 28 October from Cape Town. In 1964 she returned to the Canadian Pacific Steamships route from Liverpool to Montreal, which she maintained until 1970 when she was sold to the Shaw Savill & Albion Line and renamed *Ocean Monarch*.

She made one round sailing from Liverpool to Southampton and Australia then returned to Cammell Laird for refitting into a one-class liner. She sailed from Merseyside on 17 September 1971 but, as she was delayed due to industrial action, the Line was forced to cancel twelve cruises she was due to make that summer. She made only one Mediterranean cruise that year, leaving Southampton on 16 October.

On 5 November she left Southampton for numerous destinations. She was employed on a cruising programme out of Sydney in 1973 but, as she suffered serious mechanical problems in 1974, she returned to Britain and completed a series of cruises from Southampton. *Ocean Monarch* arrived at Southampton on her last cruise on 5 June 1975, and sailed to the shipbreakers at Kaohsiung the following week.

HMS Renown	**1968**	**Royal Navy**	**8,400 tons**
	130m x 10m	**20 knots (surface)**	**No.1,316**
		25 knots (submerged)	

In December 1962 Britain reached agreement with the United States to build its own Polaris warheads and, by 1968, the independent nuclear deterrent was ready to be deployed. HMS *Resolution* was launched on 15 September 1966 and sailed on its first patrol in 1968.

HMS Renown. *(Courtesy of Wirral Archives Service)*

In June the following year the responsibility for the United Kingdom's strategic nuclear deterrent was transferred from the Royal Air Force to the Royal Navy.

HMS *Renown* was a member of the 'Resolution' Class of submarines that were designed to carry sixteen missiles and were very similar to the American 'Lafayette' Class submarines. She was launched on 25 February 1967 and commissioned in November the following year.

Vickers at Barrow-in-Furness completed HMS *Resolution* and HMS *Repulse*, and Cammell Laird at Birkenhead built HMS *Revenge* in 1969. A pressurised water reactor and English Electric steam turbines driving one shaft powered them.

The class were armed with six 21in-forward tubes for Tigerfish torpedoes and sixteen launch tubes for Polaris A3 SLBMs, which were later redesigned to A-3TK-type and were crewed by 13 officers and 130 ratings. HMS *Renown* was upgraded in 1982 by the Chevaline programme, and decommissioned in 1995, before being laid up at Rosyth Dockyard.

HMS Onyx (S21)	**1967**	**Royal Navy**	**2,410 tons**
	89m x 8m	**17 knots**	**No.1,319**

HMS *Onyx* was built at Cammell Laird in 1967 as an 'Oberon' Class submarine. She was powered by diesel electric engines that gave her a speed of 17 knots submerged and was armed with eight 21-inch torpedo tubes forward, six forward and two aft. The aft tubes were later removed.

The 'Oberon' Class was specifically built for anti-submarine operations as they were large, very quiet, patrol vessels with good long-range sensors and underwater endurance capabilities. They were responsible for undertaking anti-submarine and anti-ship duties, forward surveillance, special forces activities, weapons development and training. In the 1980s their sonar equipment and torpedoes were updated and a missile capability extended their service to the early 1990s.

Onyx was originally ordered for the Canadian Navy and was transferred to the Royal Navy while under construction. On completion, she joined the 3rd Submarine Sqn at Faslane. HMS *Onyx* was powered by two supercharged V16-ASR1 diesel engines and two battery-powered electric engines when submerged.

The 'Oberon' Class submarines were constructed of glass fibre and alloy, which was the first time that a plastic had been used in the construction of a submarine. She was fitted with six 21in-forward torpedo tubes with a free running torpedo and wire guided Mark 24 Tigerfish torpedo. She was later fitted with the Sub-Harpoon missile and was able to deploy mines.

On her first commission in July 1969 she visited Swansea for the investiture of the Prince of Wales, and in October 1971 she had her first overhaul and refit. This lasted for two years and on her return to service she was based with the 1st Submarine Sqn in Gosport, and this commission took her to the Mediterranean and the American bicentennial celebrations in 1976.

Following her second refit she participated in European exercises and revisited various ports in the Mediterranean. Prior to being called into action in the Falklands, she was involved in a training exercise out of Portland in 1981. As part of the Falklands task force, she was responsible for special operations roles and landed special forces and gathered intelligence.

At the end of the conflict she returned to Gosport and then to Rosyth, where she had another refit and returned to the Falkland Islands as part of the South Atlantic Patrol. She also completed duties with the Canadian Navy and returned to Gosport on 14 December 1990. Following decommissioning, HMS *Onyx* became part of the Historic Warships collection at Birkenhead, and is berthed very close to where she was built.

Oberon was sold to Seaforth Ship Repairers in 1987, and was scrapped in 1991. *Ocelot* was sold to the shipbreakers in 1992 and is now preserved at a museum at Chatham Historic Dockyard; *Odin* was sold to shipbreakers in 1991; *Olympus* was sold to the Canadian Navy in 1989 and is used as a training ship at Halifax; *Onslaught* was scrapped in 1991; *Opportune* was decommissioned in 1993; *Opossum* was also decommissioned in 1993; *Orpehus* is used as the training vessel HMS *Dolphin*; *Osiris* was decommissioned in 1989 and was sold to the Canadian Navy; *Otter* was sold to the shipbreakers in 1992; *Otus* was decommissioned in 1991 and sold to the shipbreakers the following year.

HMS Onyx.

HMS Oracle.

HMS Oracle

HMS *Oracle* (S16) was another member of the class that was built at Birkenhead by Cammell Laird. She was laid down on 26 April 1960 and was launched on 26 September the following year. She is seen here on sea trials in the Irish Sea in 1962, prior to being commissioned into the Royal Navy on 14 February 1963. *Oracle* was in service in the Royal Navy until she was decommissioned in July 1993.

Spero	**1966**	**Ellerman's**	**6,916grt**
	138m x 21m	**Wilson Line**	**No.1,322**
		18 knots	

Spero was built by Cammell Laird for the Hull–Gothenburg service of the England –Sweden Line that was operated by Wilson Line, Svea Line of Stockholm and Swedish Lloyd of Gothenburg. She was Ellerman's Wilson Line's contribution to the new service and was designed to carry 408 passengers, 100 cars and 100 containers or trailers. The three ships were designed to be capable of carrying over 3,500 passengers, 1,000 cars and over 13,500 tons of cargo each week.

Spero was the first ship to be fitted with Sperry 'Gyrofin' twin-folding stabilisers and her hydraulically-operated stern door was the largest ever fitted to a British ship of this type. Her four diesel engines were designed to be controlled either from the bridge or from a soundproofed machinery control room. She was also fitted with a close circuit television system that was used as a navigation aid for docking.

When *Spero* was launched from the same slipway as *Mauretania* and HMS *Ark Royal*, she was already fitted with her four diesel engines and generating plant, gearbox, various auxiliary machinery, main switchboard, deck cranes, hatch covers and galley equipment. Some cabins were finished and the trunking from the engine room was in place for her funnel, which was the third largest ever built at the yard. Two Mirrless diesel engines developing 2,730bhp powered her, which drove the twin screws.

Following the launch, Colonel Bayley, Managing Director of Ellerman's Wilson Line, said that each of the three companies involved in the service had over 100 years' experience in providing regular services across the North Sea. The England–Sweden Line introduced radical modifications in cargo handling techniques as the ships offered facilities to importers and exporters for all kinds of freight, whether unitised by means of containers, trailers, pallets, flats or lorries.

The Marine Superintendent of Ellerman's Wilson Line, Capt. R. Tanton OBE, stressed that the design of *Spero* was extremely complex because of the necessity to build a ship to carry passengers, cars and unitised cargo. Mr R.W. Johnson, chairman of Cammell Laird, praised the co-operation the management had experienced from the unions and said that the yard was very competitive following a streamlining of costs, even against Japanese builders who were experiencing a noticeable dip in profits as their costs were mounting, both for material and labour, and they were having to revise their ideas on prices.

In 1972 *Spero* operated briefly to Zeebrugge, and was sold and renamed *Sappho* by her new Greek owners. In 2002 she was sold to Lacerta Shipping (Tanzania) Ltd, becoming *Santorini 3*, and was broken up at Alang in 2004.

Spero.

| **Ulster Queen** | **1967** | **Belfast Steamship Co.** | **4,479grt** |
| | **115m x 16m** | **17½ knots** | **No.1,323** |

Ulster Queen was built for the Belfast Steamship Co.'s Liverpool–Belfast service. Her sister, *Ulster Prince*, was built by Harland & Wolff at Belfast and ran opposite her on the nightly service, and they were the first specially built car ferries to be designed for the company. In 1971 P&O took over Coast Lines and the *Ulster Queen* and *Ulster Prince* were painted in P&O livery, but the service was closed in 1981 and both ships were offered for sale.

Ulster Queen was sold to Cypriot interests in 1982 and became *Med-Sea*, *Al-Eddin*, and *Al-Kehera* in 1987, *Poseidonia* in 1988, *La Patria* in 2000 and *Poseidonia* again in 2002.

Left: Ulster Queen.

Below: *The fitting-out basin in 1966 showing the Belfast Steamship Co.'s* Ulster Queen.

British Admiral

BP Tanker *British Admiral* arrives at the Princess Dock for overhaul in 1966. She was built the previous year for the BP Tanker Co. Ltd, and was at Birkenhead for her first annual overhaul and guarantee repairs after tank cleaning at the Rock Ferry Tanker Cleaning Installation. She was the largest vessel to enter the Mersey.

British Admiral.

Launch ticket for British Ensign.

Lion	1967	Burns &	3,333grt
	111m x 17m	Laird Line	No.1,326
		20 knots	

Lion was built for Burns & Laird Line's Ardrossan–Belfast car and passenger service. It was an all-year-round daylight service, and *Lion* was designed as a one-class ship with lounges, restaurant, cafeteria, bars and a number of passenger suites and cabins. On the main deck and folding mezzanine decks, 170 cars could be carried or a combination of cars and commercial vehicles.

Lion.

P&O took over Coast Lines in 1971 and *Lion* made her last sailing on the route on 12 February 1976. She was transferred to P&O Normandy Ferries' Dover–Boulogne service in April. The European Ferries Group took over Normandy Ferries in 1985, and Lion was used briefly on the Portsmouth–Le Havre route, prior to being sold to Greek Cypriot owners and renamed *Baroness M*.

Owned by Marlines which belonged to the Marangopolos family, the line was formed in 1982 to operate services between Ancona, Igoumenitsa and Patras, as well as services between Ancona and Cesme in Turkey.

In 1987 she was renamed *Portelet*, and *Baroness M* again in 1989, and on 24 February 1990 she was attacked by a gunboat, thirty miles off Jounich on a voyage from Larnica. One passenger was killed. She sailed from Greece to Indonesia on 24 January 1997 and was operating as the *Adinda Lestari 101* until 2004, when she was sold and broken up.

HMS Conqueror	**1971**	**Royal Navy**	**4,900 tons**
	87m x 10m	**28 knots**	**No. 1,330**

The submarine HMS *Conqueror* was launched at Birkenhead on 18 August 1969, and was commissioned in November 1971. The two other members of the class, HMS *Churchill* and HMS *Courageous*, were built by Vickers at Barrow-in-Furness. HMS *Churchill* was the last nuclear submarine to be refitted at Chatham Dockyard, and she was decommissioned on 28 February 1991.

Right: Lion *Sailing List.*

Below: *HMS* Conqueror. *(Courtesy of Wirral Archives Service)*

HMS *Conqueror* is the only nuclear-powered submarine to have engaged the enemy with torpedoes in action. She sailed from her base at Faslane on the Clyde on 3 April 1982, and took twenty-one days to get to the Falklands exclusion zone. On 30 April she reported that she had seen the Argentine heavy cruiser *General Belgrano*, which was sailing south-west of the Falkland Islands, outside the exclusion zone.

HMS *Conqueror* was ordered to sink *General Belgrano* as it was feared that she would attack from the south, as the Argentine aircraft carrier, *Vienticinco de Mayo*, was to the north of the submarine. *Conqueror* fired three torpedoes, two of which hit *General Belgrano*, and the other hit the destroyer, *Hippolite Bouchard*, that was escorting her. *General Belgrano* started to sink very quickly and was abandoned with a loss of life of 323 crew. *Conqueror* spent the rest of the conflict monitoring aircraft leaving the Argentine mainland.

She was fitted with a sub-harpoon in 1985 and collided with a yacht off the Mull of Kintyre in July 1988. On 2 August 1990 she was decommissioned at Devonport and her reactor core was removed. Her periscope is now at the Royal Navy Museum at Portsmouth.

| **Cammell Laird** | **1936** | **Cammell** | **3,290grt** |
| | **103m x 15m** | **Laird** | **17 knots** |

Cammell Laird was built in 1936 by Harland & Wolff as the *Royal Ulsterman* for the Burns & Laird Lines service from Glasgow–Belfast, She was bought by the shipyard in 1968 and renamed *Cammell Laird* for use as an accommodation vessel during the Polaris project.

She was sold to Cyprian interests in 1970 and renamed *Sounion*. On 3 March 1973 she sank at Beirut, following an underwater explosion. She was refloated the following month and arrived at Piraeus in tow on 19 September that year. She was inspected by surveyors and, because of her age and condition, it was decided that she would be sold, and she was broken up.

Cammell Laird.

Koningen Juliana.

| **Koningen Juliana** | **1968**
131m x 20m | **Zeeland**
Steamship Co. | **6,882grt**
21 knots
No. 1,331 |

Koningen Juliana was built by Cammell Laird for the Zeeland Steamship Co.'s Harwich–Hook of Holland service, and was designed to carry 1,200 passengers and 220 cars. There were two sailings a day, one night and one day, throughout the year, with additional sailings during the summer peak season. She is seen here in No.5 Drydock, prior to leaving on sea trials and sailing to Harwich, were she arrived on the 10 October 1968 for the first time. She then sailed to the Hook the following day, for final inspection and acceptance by the owners.

On 14 October she sailed on a special cruise into the North Sea with Queen Juliana on board, and she sailed on her maiden public sailing on 17 October. The service was shared with British Railways' *St George*. *St Edmund*, which was also built by Cammell Laird, joined them in 1974.

Koningen Juliana made her last sailing on the route on 7 April 1984. She was sold the following year and renamed *Tromp* to become an exhibition ship to promote Dutch products and industry. When the project was cancelled, she was sold to Moby Lines and became *Moby Prince* for use in the Mediterranean.

On 4 April 1991 she collided with the tanker *Agip Abruzzo* at Livorno, Italy, causing a fire that killed 143 people on board. The wreck of the vessel was moored at Leghorn and, on 16 May 1998, started to sink. Repairs were carried out and the wreck was towed to Aliaga, Turkey, where it arrived on 22 July 1998 for breaking up.

Cammell Laird advertisement from 1964.

HMS *Coventry* was the fourth Type-42 destroyer to enter service, and was commissioned on 10 November 1978. She was allocated to the 8th Frigate Sqn and later transferred to the newly formed 3rd Destroyer Sqn. HMS *Coventry* was deployed in the Far East with the navies of France, Pakistan, Oman and the United States. She also visited East Africa, Oman, Karachi, Singapore and Hong Kong. She made the first visit by a British warship to the Republic of China when she arrived at Shanghai in September 1980.

As she sailed home from this visit, the war between Iran and Iraq started and she was sent on patrol in the Gulf for six weeks, and returned home in December that year. She participated in a NATO exercise codenamed 'Ocean Safari' in 1981, and was based at Gibraltar early in 1982 for Operation 'Springtrain'.

In 1982 she was a member of the Falklands Task Force, which was sent from the United Kingdom to recapture the Islands from the Argentine occupation. The Falkland Islands are a group of islands in the South Atlantic which are about 400 miles from Argentina, 900 miles from Antarctica and 8,000 miles from Britain.

The British Government of the 1960s had been talking to the Argentines regarding the sovereignty of the Islands, but these talks were stopped when the Conservative Government gained power in the 1970s. Relations between the two nations had deteriorated, and in 1981 General Galtieri became president of Argentina and the invasion of the Islands took place on 2 April 1982.

On 25 May 1982, Argentine Air Force A-4B Skyhawks were given orders to target *Coventry* and *Broadsword*. *Coventry* shot down one of the aircraft on the first raid but, as the second raid appeared from behind Pebble Island, the aircraft could not be detected by her

HMS Coventry.

radar. Only one of the six bombs dropped from the aircraft hit *Broadsword*, and started a fire on board.

As the next flight attacked, *Coventry* fired a single Sea Dart missile but this missed the aircraft. *Coventry* then crossed in front of *Broadsword* and she was unable to fire. Three bombs were dropped on *Coventry*, which tore a large side of her port side and killed nineteen members of crew. The ship was engulfed in fire and the order to abandon ship was given by the captain. *Coventry* sank within 20 minutes, and *Broadsword* assisted the rescue.

The crew of *Coventry* who required medical treatment were airlifted to the hospital ship *Uganda*, and the majority of the crew were transferred to the Royal Fleet Auxiliary *Stromness*. They were later transferred to the *Queen Elizabeth 2* which sailed to Southampton, where they arrived on 11 July.

| **St Edmund** | **1974** | **British Railways** | **8,987grt** |
| | **30m x 23m** | **21 knots** | **No.1,361** |

The launch of *St Edmund* was delayed by severe weather as she was named on 13 November 1973 and did not take to the river Mersey until the following day. Work was delayed on her at the yard as Britain was operating a 'three-day-week' at the time. She was built for the Harwich to Hook of Holland service to operate as a 'night out – day back' vessel, having the capacity for 296 vehicles, 1,400 passengers on the day service and 671 overnight berths.

St Edmund finally sailed on her maiden voyage from Harwich–Hook of Holland on 19 January 1975, replacing *Avalon*, which was converted to a car ferry for the Fishguard to Rosslare service. *St Edmund* was sold in 1975 to Passtruck (Shipping) and chartered back to British Rail for the same service. In 1982 she was chartered to the Ministry of Defence to transport troops to the Falkland Islands, and was refitted at Portsmouth and sailed on 18 May.

She arrived at the Falkland Islands the day after the Argentinian troops surrendered, and was used to transport them, including their Commander-in-Chief, General Menendez, back to Puerto Madryn in Argentina. She had a helicopter pad fitted and was one of three static troop-ships berthed at Port Stanley. When she returned to Britain she was sold to the Ministry of Defence and renamed *Karen* for use as a troop carrier between the Ascension Islands and Port Stanley, as construction work on the new airport had not been finished. By 1985 she had completed twenty-seven voyages and carried 18,000 troops and workers.

Karen arrived back home in 1985 and was decommissioned at Southampton, and laid up and offered for sale. She was sold to Cenargo that year and renamed *Scirocco*. In 1986 she was chartered to Tirrenia Line of Italy and operated on the Tunisian State Line, Cotunav, between Tunis–Marseille and Genoa. She was renamed *Rozel* in 1989 to operate on the Poole to Channel Islands service for British Channel Islands Ferries. She was renamed *Scirocco* again in 1994 for Cenargo's Almeria to Nador service, eventually being replaced on this route by *Esterel* in 1997. However, in 2003 she was again on Ferrimaroc's service between Almeria–Nador and, in May 2004 she was sold to El Salam Maritime and was renamed *Santa Catherine 1*, operated by Comanav.

St Edmund *as* Rozel.

Hudson Progress. *(Courtesy of Wirral Archives Service)*

| **Hudson Progress** | **1975** | **Royal Navy** | **40,870grt** |
| | **171m x 26m** | **15 knots** | **No.1,362** |

Orangeleaf was launched as *Hudson Progress* and was renamed *Balder London* and bought by the Ministry of Defence. She was handed over to them at Falmouth on 9 March 1984 by Lloyds Industrial Leasing Ltd. She was sent to the Tyne for a major refit in 1985, and was fitted with gantries and other equipment to enable her to be able to replenish naval ships at sea. She was also fitted with extra accommodation and new navigational equipment and electronics, and is the third tanker to bear the name.

She entered service with the Ministry of Defence with the main role to resupply warships at sea with furnace oil, diesel and aviation fuel, and to make bulk movements of oil between Ministry of Defence depots. She is capable of refuelling two ships at once and in rough weather, the refuelling hose can be trailed astern and lifted up by the receiving warship.

Orangeleaf has a crew of fifty-six, which includes nineteen officers and is designed to carry 22,000 cubic metres of diesel and 3,800 cubic metres of Avcat. She is propelled by two Crossley-Pielstick Type 14PC2V diesel engines connected to one propeller, and is equipped with 20mm and 7.62mm guns.

In 2003 she was operating as the Arabian Gulf Ready Tanker and is scheduled to return to complete this tour of duty in 2005. Her main role was to support Royal Naval vessels, and she has also refuelled warships of allied and friendly nations, from large American aircraft carriers to smaller ships from Australia, Canada, the Netherlands, France and Oman. She has been based in Dubai but has also visited Kuwait, Doha, Fujairah, Salalh and Jebel Ali.

| **HMS Liverpool** | **1982** | **Royal Navy** | **4,820 tons** |
| | **125m x 14m** | **30 knots** | **No.1,374** |

Lady Strathcona, the wife of the Minister of State for Defence, launched HMS *Liverpool* on 25 September 1980. She is a Type-42 Destroyer (Batch 2) that is armed with the Twin Sea Dart medium range defence missile system and has a COGAG (combined Gas and Gas) turbines propulsion system.

HMS Liverpool.

The main role of the Type-42 destroyers is to provide anti-air defence for a task force in an anti-air warfare capacity, and to confront surface and anti-submarine targets. HMS *Sheffield* was launched in 1971 and was the first of thirteen sister ships, and two of the class were also built for the Argentine Navy.

They are powered by two Rolls Royce gas turbines for cruising and two Olympus gas turbines, which give a speed of 31 knots, and are armed with British Aerospace surface-to-air Sea Dart missile systems. *Manchester, Gloucester, Edinburgh* and *York* are slightly longer than her sisters, which gives them more room for special equipment.

Type-42 destroyers took part in the Falklands War, and *Sheffield* and *Coventry* were lost during that conflict. *Gloucester* and *Cardiff* participated in the Gulf War in 1991, and were responsible for the destruction of a number of anti-aircraft batteries, minesweepers, landing craft and missile patrol vessels. They were also on duties in the Caribbean, West Indies and the South Atlantic, working with the United States Drug Enforcement Agency, and *Southampton* and *Liverpool* helped at Montserrat in 1990.

HMS Edinburgh	**1985**	**Royal Navy**	**4,675 tons**
	141m x 15m	**30 knots**	**No.1,375**

HMS *Edinburgh* was laid down in July 1980 at Birkenhead, and was launched by Mrs Anne Heseltine on 14 April 1983. She is powered by two Tyne gas turbines for cruising and two Olympus gas turbines which give her a speed of just over 30 knots.

The comprehensive radar and sonar suite imputs into the ship's computer system to allow an effective use of her weapons, Sea Dart anti-air or anti-surface missile system, for

HMS Edinburgh.

close range defence and policing roles. She also has a multi-role Lynx helicopter capable of deploying missiles and torpedoes, and has electronic warfare and communications equipment, along with data links to exchange computer information with other ships.

| **HMS Campbeltown** | **1989** | **Royal Navy** | **5,300 tons** |
| | **148m x 15m** | **30 knots** | **No.1,378** |

HMS *Campbeltown* was the third Type-22 Batch 3 class frigate equipped with anti-surface, anti-submarine and anti-aircraft weapons systems. She was launched on 7 October 1987 and entered service in the Royal Navy in 1989. She is armed with a 114mm-(4.5in) MK 8 gun, Goalkeeper close-in weapons system, Sea Wolf anti-missile system, 2 Quad Harpoon missile launchers, 2x20mm-close range guns and NATO Seagnat Decoy Launchers.

The ship's bell from the first HMS *Campbeltown* was presented to the town of Campbeltown in Pennsylvania, USA, at the end of the Second World War, as a token of gratitude to the United States for the lend-lease programme. In 1988, the townspeople of Campbeltown voted to lend the bell to the current HMS *Campbeltown* for the duration of her service in the Royal Navy, after which it would be returned to America. HMS *Campbeltown* also has strong links with Campbeltown, Argyll, in Scotland.

HMS Campbeltown. *(Courtesy of Wirral Archives Service)*

HMS Unseen. *(Courtesy of Wirral Archives Service)*

HMS Unseen	**1991**	**Royal Navy**	**2,200 tons**
	70m x 8m	**20 knots**	**No.1,379**

HMS *Unseen* was launched at the yard in September 1989, and was commissioned in 1991. There are four submarines in the 'Upholder Class', three of which – *Unseen, Ursula* and *Unicorn* – were built by Cammell Laird, with *Upholder* being built by Vickers Shipbuilding & Engineering Ltd. They were fitted with two Paxman Valenta diesel engines, two 1.4 GEC alternators and one GEC electric motor.

In 1979 a decision was made to replace the 'Oberon' Class submarines, and the Type-2400 was revealed. They were designed for reconnaissance in shallow waters, and the initial plan to construct twelve vessels was reduced to ten and, following the 1990/91 Defence Review, it was cut to four. They were commissioned just when the Cold War was ending when their reconnaissance role was no longer required and the Admiralty also decided to concentrate on nuclear powered submarines. The four submarines were taken out of service in 1994 and laid up in Barrow-in-Furness, awaiting a buyer.

On 2 July 1998, agreement was reached with the governments of Britain and Canada for the lease of the four vessels for a period of eight years at a cost of £254 million. The four submarines were refitted and recommissioned into the Royal Canadian Navy. *Upholder* became *Chicoutinu, Unseen* became *Victoria, Ursula* became *Corner Brook* and *Unicorn* became *Windsor*.

Corner Brook suffered overheating of her propulsion systems in 2003 and was sent to the Naval Base in Halifax, where it was discovered that the saltwater intake valves were clogged with mussels from the bottom of the Halifax harbour. *Chicoutinu* was rolled out of the Devonshire Dock Hall at Barrow on 1 October 2003. She was due to undertake trails and was handed over to the Canadian Navy in Spring 2004.

HMCS *Chicoutini* suffered a serious fire and was disabled on her delivery voyage to Canada in October 2004, and was towed back to Faslane in Scotland for repairs to be completed.

Other local titles published by The History Press

Mersey Shipping Remembered
IAN COLLARD

A record of a time of change and upheaval in the life of a maritime centre and one that will be remembered by everyone involved in the shipping and associated industries on Merseyside. *Mersey Shipping Remembered* provides a nostalgic reminder of the heyday of Liverpool's long maritime history.
0 7524 2815 2

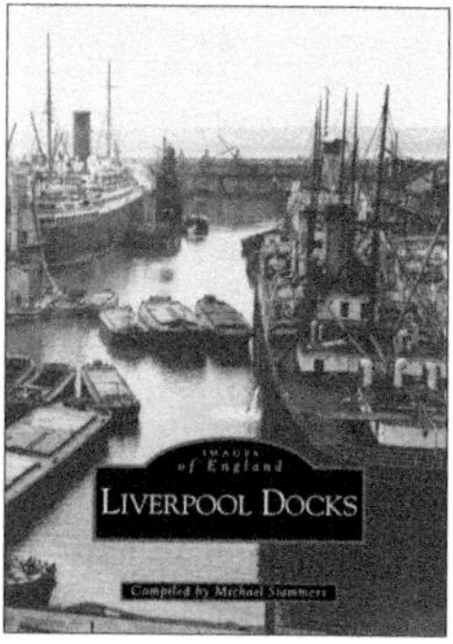

Liverpool Docks
MICHAEL STAMMERS

The story of Liverpool is, in many ways, the story of its docks. With contemporary illustrations of people, ships, buildings and machinery, Michael Stammers chronicles not just the rise and fall of Mersey shipping but also the way the docks have bounced back. Redevelopment, restoration and new modes of commerce have put Liverpool's docks back in the black, albeit looking very different to the port of sixty years ago.
0 7524 1712 6

Mersey Shipping The Twilight Years
IAN COLLARD

This is a book about life in a great maritime port of the 1960s. The photographs from the period show a busy, vibrant scene of commercial and industrial activity. Sadly, it is a scene that has gone forever, but as Liverpool's dock buildings take on new roles and the city moves into the twenty-first century, we can at least look and remember the sea-going commerce that made Liverpool great.
0 7524 1732 0

Cunard A Photographic History
JANETTE MCCUTCHEON

Celebrating its 165th anniversary in 2005, Cunard has had its ups and downs and is now building another new Queen to follow in the footsteps of its illustrious sisters.

Using over 200 illustrations, many previously unpublished, Janette McCutcheon tells the story of Cunard from its early beginnings to the present day.
0 7524 3001 7

If you are interested in purchasing other books published by The History Press, or in case you have difficulty finding any of our books in your local bookshop, you can also place orders directly through our website
www.thehistorypress.co.uk